ROCK CLIMBS
OF
SOUTHWEST UTAH
& THE ARIZONA STRIP

by Todd Goss

Bobbi Bensman on Redneck (5.12b)
Photo by Jim Thornburg

Rock Climbs of Southwest Utah and the Arizona Strip

by Todd Goss
©2000 by Sharp End Publishing, LLC. All rights reserved. This book or any part thereof may not be reproduced in any form without written permission from the publisher.

ISBN # 1-892540-02-9

For a complete list of titles available from Sharp End Publishing, please write to PO Box 1613, Boulder, CO 80306 or e-mail at inforock@aol.com.

Sharp End Publishing is always looking for new material. Please send queries to the address or email address above.

Cover photos: Katie Brown on Fossil of a Man, Phalanx of Will by Jorge Visser; inset photo of Scott Frye on F-Dude, Virgin River Gorge by Jim Thornburg.

READ THIS BEFORE USING THIS GUIDE BOOK

Dedication

To Erin Jones...friend, partner, companion, critic, builder of trails, bolter of routes, hauler of ropes, adventurer, discoverer, prophet and sage. Thanks for your support and understanding.

To my dad for 38 years of looking out for me, and for instilling a healthy sense of cynicism.

To Darl Biniaz, climbing partner extraordinaire and fellow intelligentsia.

Acknowledgments

It often seems silly to take credit for writing a book like this when so many other people help with it. But as P.J. O'Rourke said, "To them goes the credit. I'll take the money."

Greatest thanks goes to the many climbing partners who have put up with being photographed at ridiculous hours of the day, and shanghaied out to obscure climbing areas to do "research" when they would rather be doing laps at Chuckawalla. Darl Biniaz, Lyle and Rich Hurd, Bo Beck, Michal and Jen Nad, Mike and Elizabeth Tupper, Rob Foster, Ian Horn, Jesse Lee, and Andy Betzhold. Thanks for tolerating both my tirades and intestinal discord.

Without the many climbers who have been generous with route info this book would fit in your wallet. Thanks to: Todd Perkins, Jorge Visser, Jeff Baldwin, Lee Logston, Lange Jefferies, Boone Speed, Jeff Pederson, Jeremy Brown, Randy Leavitt, Tyler Phillips, Troy Anderson, Tim Duck, and Glen Griscome for the beta.

Thanks to Doug and Bo at the Outdoor Outlet who have let me get away with murder in regards to my work schedule, and who have made significant contributions to the quantity of climbing in this area.

Special thanks to John Ibach and Kendall Farnsworth of Snow Canyon State Park, and to Bill Madder of the Red Cliffs Desert Reserve. As land managers of state parks and agencies in this region, they have been very accommodating towards climbers on the cliffs they manage.

"Choose your friends carefully. Your enemies will choose you."
-Yassir Arafat

TABLE OF CONTENTS

TABLE OF CONTENTS

TABLE OF CONTENTS

INTRODUCTION

Southwest Utah is a veritable dog's breakfast of rock climbing opportunities. With exposed rock in every direction, of every description, and every composition, it offers the greatest concentration of climbing variety in the country. Sandstone, limestone, basalt, welded tuff, and quartzite conglomerate cobbles are the big swing-sets in our backyard, and if you have quickdraws or cams in your toy box you will certainly have a good time.

One of the problems facing the visiting climber with limited time is choosing from so many areas in such a small region. A good place to start is choosing what kind of rock you would like to climb on, and narrow it down to grades and type of climbing from there.

This guide contains route information for more than 40 areas in southwestern Utah and the Arizona Strip, describing nearly a thousand routes. No area is more than 100 miles from the center of St. George, though St. George may be 100 years behind other areas.

Most of the areas covered in this guide are bolted sport crags, but several traditional climbing areas are also included. This is not intended as a slight or bias against traditional climbing. It is a simple reflection of what is out there, and excepting Zion there aren't many developed crack areas around here. I have elected to leave Zion National Park out of this edition for reasons of brevity, and as it has received adequate coverage elsewhere.

Finally, do not read this book without a healthy sense of humor and appreciation for the ridiculous. We should always remember that what we do isn't nuclear science or medical research — we're just climbing rocks. Lighten up and have fun out there. Hopefully this book will help you do just that.

Todd Goss

"Idealism is what precedes experience; cynicism is what follows"
-David T. Wolf

USING THIS GUIDE

This book is arranged into twelve general regions, each of which has a number of crags in that area. The areas are listed in order of progressively greater driving time from the town of St. George.

Each route has a brief description of the features, or the climbing style offered by the route. I have endeavored to be both brief but descriptive, and offer helpful information without divulging the crux sequences or even mentioning the crux if at all possible.

RATINGS

This guide uses the intergalactic rating system whereby the square root of Pi is multiplied by each climbers height and weight, and divided by the distance in centimeters between their eyeballs. OK, seriously this book uses the Yosemite Decimal System common to most North American climbing areas. The ratings here may be characterized as somewhat soft by Joshua Tree standards (Sandbag City), or somewhat harsh by western Ohio standards (where 5.10 is tying your shoes) — which means the ratings are just about right. Because the ratings are a consensus of opinion, they are by nature subjective and should be taken as such.

On the climbs in this guide which require the placement of removable protection an attempt has been made to describe the size of pro required. These routes may also be accompanied by an R or X rating if the protection is difficult to place or nonexistent, respectively.

Each route is also given a quality rating based on how much spray I've had to listen to about each and every move on them.

***= An area classic, worth the approach even if it is the only route to do.

** = A very good route worth the hike in, but doesn't justify scary approaches through death talus. Worth about three minutes of spray at medium volume with minimal hand gestures.

* = A route worth doing but probably not worth a long approach. Generally elicits a shrug and brief description of the coolest move.

No Stars = A route not worth the trouble, or a new route where no one but the first ascentionist has had the chance to spray.

ETHICS

Thought by many to mean those old battle cries during the Bolt Wars. In today's world, ethics are more likely to include such actions as picking up someone else's trash, not stealing their draws, not disturbing nesting raptors, not hammering bolt hangers flat, and not chipping edges or drilling finger pockets. Ethics are the moral restrictions we impose upon ourselves because it is right to do so. As climbing becomes ever more popular, ethics will play a greater role in our continued privilege to climb on some public lands. Land managers don't care a bit about questions of style, but nothing can get an area closed faster than a group of unethical climbers.

"To hell with world peace, try visualizing using your turn signal"
-bumper sticker

GETTING TO ST. GEORGE

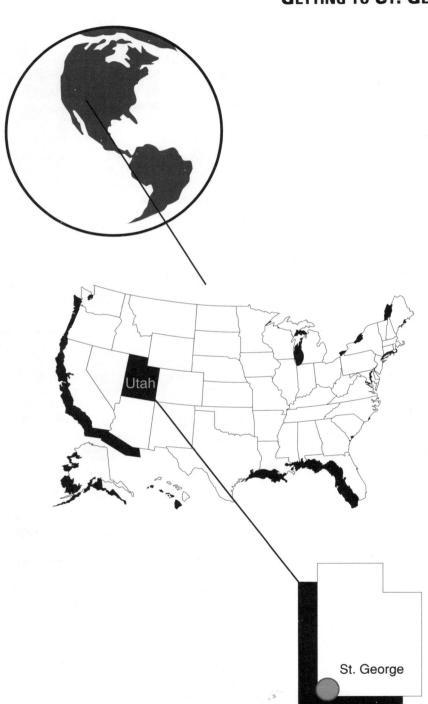

St. George

UTAH STATE MAP

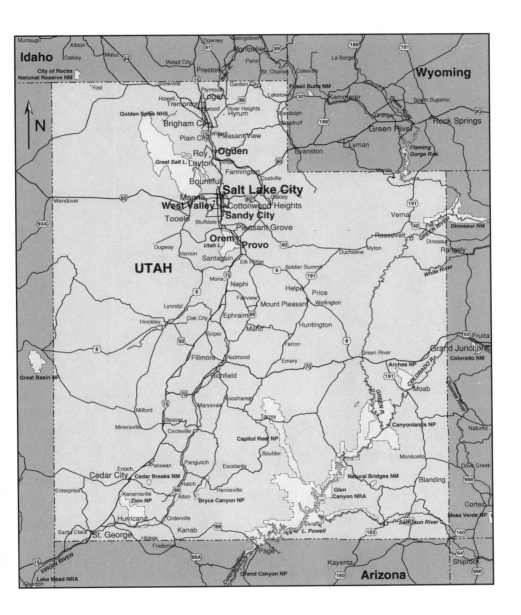

SOUTHWEST UTAH & THE ARIZONA STRIP

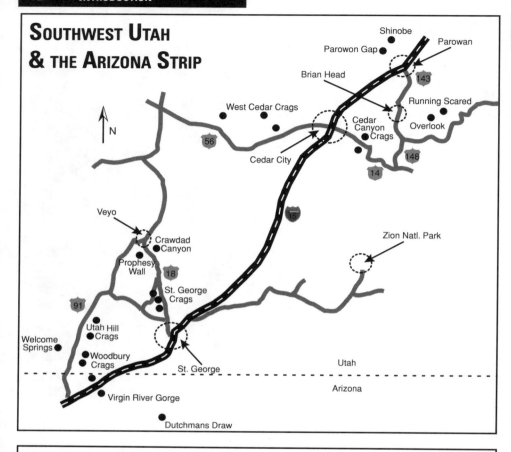

Shinobe

Parowon Gap

Parowan

Brian Head

143

West Cedar Crags

Running Scared

Cedar Canyon Crags

Overlook

148

Cedar City

14

N

56

Veyo

Crawdad Canyon

Prophesy Wall

18

St. George Crags

91

Utah Hill Crags

Welcome Springs

Woodbury Crags

St. George

Zion Natl. Park

Utah

Arizona

Virgin River Gorge

Dutchmans Draw

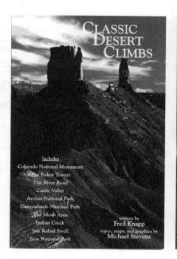

CLIMBING HISTORY

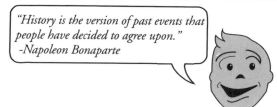

"History is the version of past events that people have decided to agree upon."
-Napoleon Bonaparte

The first climbers in this part of the country were undoubtedly the Anasazi and Freemont cultures of the early 1100's. A visit to these sites would confirm their climbing ability. Though several of their routes were blatantly chipped, this era was pre-sticky rubber, (in fact pre-shoes and pre-Columbian as well) so some lapses of style are understandable.

The next group of climbers to colonize the region were the Mormon pioneers. Growing cotton and stealing land from the Native Americans elicited greater interest than climbing, and excepting some general graffiti with wagon wheel grease, the cliffs remained unmolested.

The modern era of climbing is said to have begun with the ascent of the Great White Throne in Zion National Park in 1961. The unexpected climbability of the soft sandstone sparked a slow but steady stream of new routes in the park, though little word of these endeavors leaked beyond the canyon walls.

As the painters pants of the 70's gave way to the shiny lycra of the 80's, climbers began to notice the bounty of climbable rock lying untouched around the region. The delicate desert varnish of Snow Canyon State Park was discovered to offer excellent face climbing and several formations received their first routes.

By 1989, as standards improved and attitudes changed, climbers from Salt Lake City began stopping and climbing in the Virgin River Gorge instead of driving right through to Red Rocks. The broad acceptance of bolting on rappel opened the way for new possibilities and several areas were soon discovered and developed.

In the mid 90's interest expanded to other rock types in the region. Quality basalt, limestone, conglomerate and welded tuff areas provide the incredible variety this area is famed for. The nation's largest private climbing park was founded in Crawdad Canyon's during this period.

If history is any guide, the climbers of the 21st century will again take a fresh look, challenge the current paradigm and make their own unique contribution to our rich and diverse sport.

GEOLOGY

The landscape of southwestern Utah is a geological stew. Take a few million years of detritus accretion, add some precipitate, and metamorphose on low for three eons. Fold, wrinkle, then fault, and top with several lacolithic orogenies and serve. Salt and pepper to taste.

St. George sits in a depressed basin at the north end of the Shivwits Plateau. The vast Hurricane Fault runs just east of town, and separates the various layer cake sandstones of the Colorado Plateau from the basin and range limestone formations to the west. The Pine Valley Range rises to the north of town, and basalt flows spill away from the range in three directions. To the north and east of the Hurricane Fault, hot ash flows compressed into volcanic tuff, and lava flowed from a similar event. West of Parowan, river deposition built layers of conglomerate sandstone with quartzite cobbles the size of pumpkins.

In layman's terms this means you can't swing a cat without hitting some type of climbable rock. Previously swung cats may be adopted at the city animal shelter.

BIOLOGY

Three of America's great arid regions come together in southwestern Utah. The Great Basin and Mojave Deserts, and Colorado Plateau all intersect roughly within a 20 mile radius of St. George. Each region has distinctive flora and fauna with transitional zones in between.

The Mojave Desert is dominated by creosote bushes, yucca, and low cactus species. The Joshua Tree, trademark species of the Mojave, reaches its northern limit in the Utah Hills west of town. Reptiles and mammals here avoid the intense heat in summer by being mostly nocturnal. (Local climbers avoid it by being lazy, and staying inside in the air-conditioning).

The Great Basin desert is typified by Pinon pine and Juniper trees surrounded by empty miles of sage and rabbit brush. Colder than the lower Mojave, it supports a wide variety of fauna.

The Colorado Plateau is classified as semi-arid, and receives more rainfall than the other regions. Dissected by deep and often surprisingly lush canyons, plant and animal life here is often dictated by elevation, rainfall, and soil quality.

RAPTOR ETIQUETTE

As climbers we are not the only inhabitants of the vertical environment. We share this vertical world with the species that make these cliffs their home. Eagles, hawks, falcons, and even cliff swallows and canyon wrens have squatter's rights on the cliff faces we covet. Though some of these species may be more tolerant of boorish guests than others, it is incumbent upon us to act responsibly and respectfully when climbing in their neighborhood.

Most species of birds court and mate in the spring, and then begin to select sites where they will nest and raise young. Climbing activity in these areas may force the pair to select less optimal sites than ones where climbing activity is taking place. This may result in increased chance for predation, overheating, and desiccation of eggs or young.

Once the nest site is selected and eggs are laid, climbing activity in the area of the nest may cause especially sensitive birds to abandon the site, or at a minimum cause the nest to be unoccupied for the period of time that the climbers are present. This may again create less than optimal conditions for the incubation of the eggs and the care and feeding of the young. *Signs of raptor disturbance include:*
- The birds taking avoidance flights out of the nest and circling around.
- Raptors screaming at climbers too close to the nest area.
- Raptors dive-bombing climbers who are too close to the nest area.
If any of the above behavior is observed you are causing disturbance to the nesting pair present and should relocate your activities to another area.

Several areas in this guidebook are historical nesting sites and as such are seasonally closed to climbing by managing agencies. These periods are usually from January through February and May through June. There are also other areas that have not received official closures but still have active raptor nests. We climbers need to voluntarily restrict ourselves from visiting these areas when doing so has a negative impact on the raptors. Doing anything else is not only ill-mannered and provincial, but may cause more severe restrictions to be implemented in the future.

OBJECTIVE HAZARDS

The desert regions of the world have always been characterized as unforgiving and rugged. Anyplace where you can be bitten by a snake and die shortly thereafter is pretty unforgiving in my book. But deadly snakes are not the only dangers, there are numerous other hazards out there just waiting to send you home in the meat wagon.

Scorpions: Not real deadly ones like in the Sonoran, but big and ugly. You could die of fright if one crawled down your pants.

Spiders: Black Widow and Brown Recluse pose a greater threat to young children and geezers than to alert climbers, but their bite would certainly ruin your day.

Cactus: Everything in the desert bites or stings — even the vegetables.

Snakes: Several varieties of rattlesnake inhabit the region. The Mojave Green is especially venomous, aggressive, and territorial. If you are bitten by any snake, kill it and bring it to the hospital. Not all snakes inject venom or full loads of venom with every bite, but go to the hospital anyway.

Rockfall: Sandstone is in the process of becoming just plain sand. It is soft and often breaks without notice. Several areas recently developed have not had the traffic to remove loose rock. A helmet may be a good idea in these areas.

Lightning: Lots of people die every year from lightning strikes. An especially dumb place to be is on the side of a cliff with a bunch of metal doo-dads hanging off of your body. Summer thunderstorms occur with great regularity in the Brian Head area, at times coming with little or no warning. Be prepared to seek shelter.

Flash Floods: Narrow canyon areas are prone to flash flooding. Use caution when climbing in places where it would be difficult to get out of in a hurry. It doesn't have to be raining where you are for a flash flood to occur. The drainage basins that feed the canyon you may be in could be miles away.

Haunta Virus: Dust from deer mouse poop can carry the deadly Haunta Virus. Try not to breathe.

Humans: There are rednecks with guns out there too. Talk nice to them, and they might not shoot you.

Plague and Locusts: Just kidding.

"The secret of life is honesty and fair dealing. If you can fake that, you've got it made."
- Groucho Marx

WEATHER

Southwestern Utah is a bonafide four season climbing area. Contrary to popular opinion it is possible to climb on any one of the crags listed in this guide in the middle of the summer without getting heat stroke in the process. However, summers are hot with afternoon temperatures routinely well over 100 degrees in the shade. The trick during this time of year is climb early or at higher elevation crags. Spring brings warm temperatures (70's) around March, but also unpredictable weather patterns with wind and rain possible. Fall usually begins around mid-September, and usually offers stable weather with 70 to 80 degree temps by October. Winters are hard to predict, with long periods of rain or even snow in the higher altitudes. On the frequent sunny winter days, high temps range from the 40's to the mid-60's.

NEW ROUTES AND RED TAGS

This information may come as a shock to the casual climber – and will be an absolute epiphany to many of the locals – but all the bolts sticking out of the rocks at your favorite crag had to be paid for by some schmuck who probably couldn't afford it in the first place. Said schmuck then pawned his TV to buy a Bosch, worked at Wendy's to get a hammer, and spent what remained of his or her free time cleaning dirt out of pockets, removing death flakes, and inhaling enough rock dust to make black lung disease seem like a good time by comparison. These schmucks risked scorpion stings, rattlesnake bites, and lightning strikes to set up the route, then spent weeks or sometimes years attaining the knowledge, attitude, and fitness to finally send the thing. All that for a route some climbers could do one-handed in oversized bowling shoes.

Without people willing to make this kind of sacrifice and contribution to the quality of climbing in this region we would be making reservations six months in advance to climb Cave Crack.

A new route is a gift of time, money, and vision to the climbing community. We can show our appreciation by honoring the first ascent principle, and by respecting their efforts by staying off red tagged projects. The first ascent principle simply means aspiring to climb the route in the same manner as the first ascentionist. This means not adding or removing bolts, chipping holds, or drilling pockets.

A red tag on the first bolt of a route indicates that the route has yet to receive a first ascent, and is someone's project. It makes no difference whether the route is 5.5 or 5.15. It means something to the person who put the time and resources into creating it, and he or she should have as much time as necessary to complete the process.

Recently, several climbers have begun to ignore red tags. Instead of doing the hard work of developing new areas and routes of their own, they have begun looting the projects of others. This is both morally wrong and contrary to the spirit of first ascents. I will not support this behavior by giving first ascent credit to route looters in this guidebook, and would encourage other guidebook authors to do the same.

"Yes I do think there ought to be a time limit on a project—my lifetime!"
-Mike Tupper

St. George

As a base of operations in the war against gravity, the city of St. George makes an admirable headquarters. Four grocery stores, restaurants offering everything from Chinese to Mexican, two bagel shops, four laundromats, and even a couple of coffee shops.

"It's an island babe. If you don't bring it here, you won't find it here."
- Harrison Ford in 6 Days and 7 Nights

But this is Utah where the state flag should be a rectangle of beige. So be prepared for mono-culturalisim, one liquor store, 3.2% beer, 10 golf courses, empty streets (and crags) on Sundays, and an otherwise bleak social scene.

Groceries
Smiths- Bluff St.
Lin's- Sunset Blvd.
Harmons- 700 South
Albertsons- Bluff St.

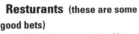

Resturants (these are some good bets)
Irmita's- Mexican- Bluff St.
Cafe Rio- Mexican- Promenade Mall
The Bear Claw- American- Main St.
J.J. Hunan- Chinese- Ancestor Square
Pasta Factory- Pasta- Ancestor Square
Scaldoni's- Italian- Sunset Blvd.
Luigi's- Italian- St. George Blvd.

Coffee Shops
The Bean Scene- St. George Blvd.
Jazzy Java - Bluff St.

Alcohol
State liquor store. Sunset Blvd. Call for hours. (11-7 generally)

Other Entertainments
For wholesomness, in quanities capable of killing a normal human, try the **Family Fun Center** just off Bluff Street. Five movie theaters.
Mesquite NV. 35 miles south (activities classified as illegal in Utah).

Equipment
The Outdoor Outlet-
1062 E. Tabernacle
Hurst- Bluff St.

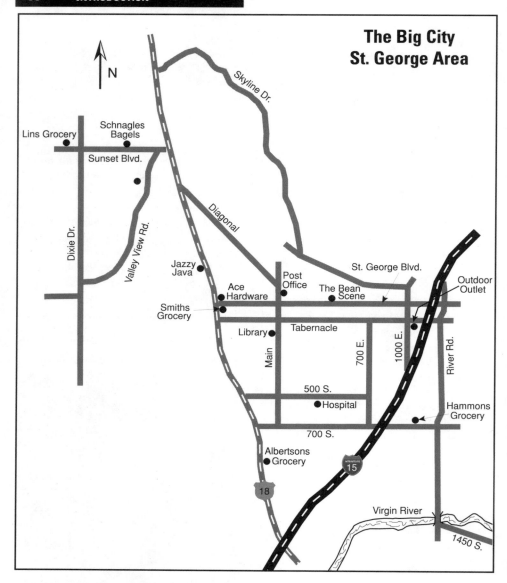

The Big City
St. George Area

N

Skyline Dr.

Lins Grocery

Schnagles Bagels

Sunset Blvd.

Dixie Dr.

Valley View Rd.

Diagonal

Jazzy Java

Ace Hardware

Smiths Grocery

Post Office

The Bean Scene

St. George Blvd.

Outdoor Outlet

Library

Tabernacle

Main

700 E.

1000 E.

River Rd.

500 S.

Hospital

Hammons Grocery

700 S.

Albertsons Grocery

18

INTERSTATE 15

Virgin River

1450 S.

INJURIES / ACCIDENTS

As with other climbing areas where and how you get injured will have a great bearing on the speed of rescue or assistance available. 911 is the local number to summon assistance or notify the hospital that you're on the way.

Several of the areas in this book are in remote enough locations that emergency assistance would be hours away, and climbers using these areas have an added responsibility to be prepared to help themselves should an accident occur. This is probably a good mindset to have in any area you are climbing in regardless of the remoteness.

Dixie Regional Medical Center:
Located on 544 South 400 East (435) 634-4000.

ST. GEORGE CRAGS

Todd Perkins on The Cross (5.12b)

CHUCKAWALLA WALL

The first wall in the St. George area developed as a sport climbing crag. Chuckawalla was pioneered by local climber Jorge Visser who cleaned and bolted the first three routes in late 1993. Described by Randy Leavitt as "a road cut," layers of choss were removed to reveal hidden pockets, and edges that make for enjoyable and fingertip friendly climbing. With the addition of some warm-up routes on the right hand side and the eventual filling in of the gaps between the existing routes by Visser, Todd Perkins, Michal Nad, Wade Widdeson, Mike Tupper and Todd Goss, Chuckawalla is now quite thoroughly bolted. In fact, endless variations are now possible such as Rob Harker's rope drag traverse, starting on Second Coming and ending at Mecca's anchors. This has lead one local to comment,"One more bolt in Chuckawalla and the whole damn thing may just fall down." The nature of the stone also makes the grades get harder from year to year as once positive edges and pockets become less so. We hope that as this happens we may all become 5.14 climbers. Chuckawalla is a great training wall with excellent opportunities to train on finger friendly holds until failure.

Season

This is a truly year round crag. Even on the hottest summer day climbing is possible until noon as the wall is in deep shade. Winter afternoons are frequently shirtless affairs as the wall blocks the prevailing winds and soaks up the sun.

Access

Drive 1.0 mile north of the Sunset Blvd. intersection on Bluff St. (Rt. 18) and turn left into a pullout and park. Cross the paved bike path and the fence at the step over provided. Walk 100 meters down the road and the crag is on the right.

Note: Chuckawalla Wall is part of the Red Cliffs Reserve. This area has been set aside as habitat conservation for the desert tortoise and other threatened or endemic species. We may climb on this and other formations in this preserve as long as our activities do not affect these species, or their habitat requirements. Please act responsibly when using this area. Though a party spot for years, do not start fires or in any other way degrade the surroundings. Do not allow your behavior to adversely affect the good will that local climbers enjoy with the agencies that manage these areas.

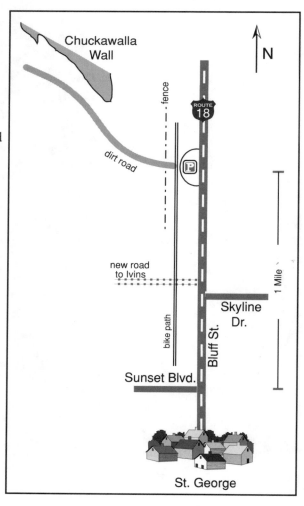

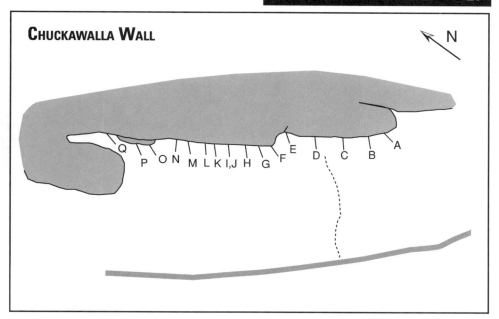

CHUCKAWALLA ROUTES

A. Apostasy 5.10a**
T. Goss
Five bolts lead through pockets and underclings to chains. (45')

B. Dirtbag 5.10a**
J. Visser
Pull through the overhang on big holds past four bolts to anchor. (45')

C. Tombstone Bullets 5.10c/d**
T. Goss
Sinker pockets lead to cruxy bulge. Five bolts, rap hangers. (45')

D. Sand-witch 5.11b*
J. Visser
Reachy pockets lead to a committing move at chains. Five bolts. (45')

E. Second Coming Variation 5.11c*
M. Nad
Shares first three bolts with F then right to chains. Six bolts. (55')

F. Second Coming 5.12a***
J. Visser
Slopers and pockets lead to wild overhanging prow. Seven bolts. (60')

G. Happiness is Coming 5.11d**
M. Nad
Nice pocket route through bulge on good holds. Seven bolts, shares anchors with route H. (60')

H. Still Waiting 5.12a**
J. Visser
Pocket climbing to overhang on good holds. Six bolts to chains. (60')

I. Say Your Prayers 5.11d
J. Visser
I pray the Lord this crimp I keep. Six bolts to chains. (60')

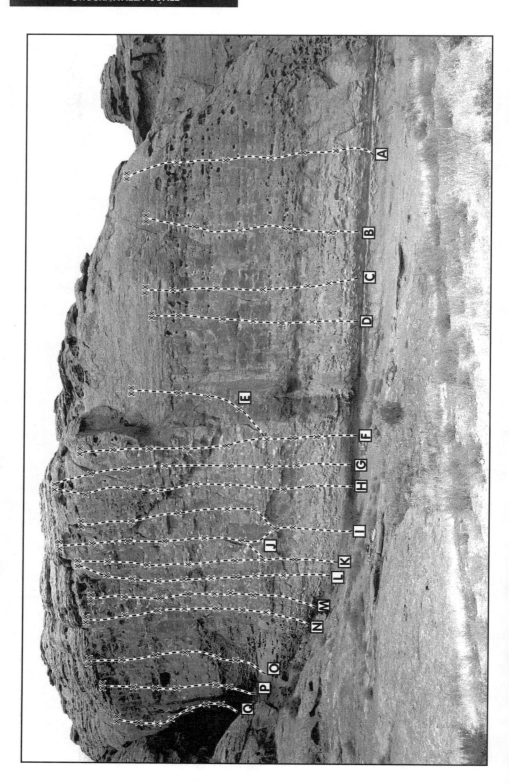

J. As the Jerks Fly 5.12a**
M. Nad, J. Nad
Sport rappellers used to come here and kick off the holds until their anchor "disappeared". Starts on K or I. Seven bolts total to chains. (55')

K. Pilgrimage 5.12a***
J. Visser
One of the best on the crag. Six bolts through sustained pocket climbing and a committing finish at the chains. (50')

L. Vertical Smile 5.12a*
T. Perkins, L. Hopkinson
Crimps in a waterstreak. Eight bolts to common chain anchor with K. (50')

M. Mecca 5.11c**
W. Widdeson, T. Goss
Pockets and slopey
crux past six bolts to
chains. (50')

N. As the Crows Fly 5.11b***
J. Visser, T. Perkins
A great route for laps,
sustained pockets past
six bolts to chains.
(50')

O. The Cross 5.12b**
J. Visser
Good holds to crimpy
crux. Route is 11d if
climbed to the right of
the bolts. Five bolts to
chains. (50')

P. The Garden of Eden 5.10d**
T. Perkins
Five bolts past slopey
bulge to chains. (50')

Q. Three Bars Black 5.13b**
M. Tupper, E. Tupper
Cross-throughs and
dyno's lead to a hand
foot match in pocket.
Six bolts to open
coldshuts. (45')

Rob Foster on Pilgrimage (5.12a)

"I'm climbing like old people screw — slow and jerky."
- Mike Tupper

THE BLACK ROCKS

The first basalt area to be developed in the St. George area, The Black Rocks has become one of the most popular climbing areas in southwestern Utah. This is due to its proximity to town as well as its easy access, range of grades and user friendliness for toproping.

Ron Olvesky first looked at The Black Rocks in the late 80's and actually put in a couple of rivets and toproped a crack, but dismissed the area as being too short for technical climbing. In 1994 Todd Goss and Anthony Jones climbed several of the cracks on the sunny side, and Goss began setting up toprope anchors with pitons in cracks and getting his father to hand drill the first 1/2" bolt (a three hour process). In 1995 Goss purchased a Bosch, began route development in earnest, a process fueled by the arrival of prolific first ascentionists Mike and Elizabeth Tupper. Two years later over 40 routes lined both sides of this small but thoroughly enjoyable canyon. With grades from 5.7 to 5.13b this is one of the best crags around for climbers of all abilities.

Season

The Black Rocks are climbable year round with winter, spring and fall being most comfortable. Summer days on the sunny side can actually melt the soles of your shoes, but the north facing side of this east-west canyon is climbable until noon.

Access

Drive north on Bluff St. (Rt. 18) 2.0 miles past the Sunset Blvd intersection. A yellow "Falling Rocks" caution sign is on the right, and the road starts to descend to cross over the canyon. On the left a dirt road is seen leaving the asphalt and climbing up a hill. You may drive up this road and park prior to the paved bike path or pull off on the right and park well off the road on the shoulder. Hike to the top of the hill and locate the step-through section of the fence that marks the boundry of the Red Cliffs Preserve. Cross over the fence at this point and follow the obvious trail to the rim of the canyon and downclimb the boulders into the canyon. A left turn will take you to the shady side. For the sunny side, continue down the trail to the stream bed. Cross the wash and follow the trail to the sunny side wall.

Note: Many of the routes require accessing the cliff top and setting up anchors with biners and slings. Some of the leadable routes have anchors that are inaccessible from the top but many have chains which drape over the edge of the cliff. Some of the anchors are open coldshuts. Use caution when approaching the top of the route. Several inexperienced climbers have topped out on these anchors with the rope coming out of the top of the shuts.

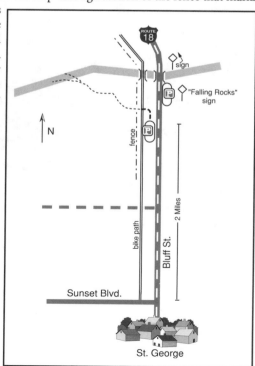

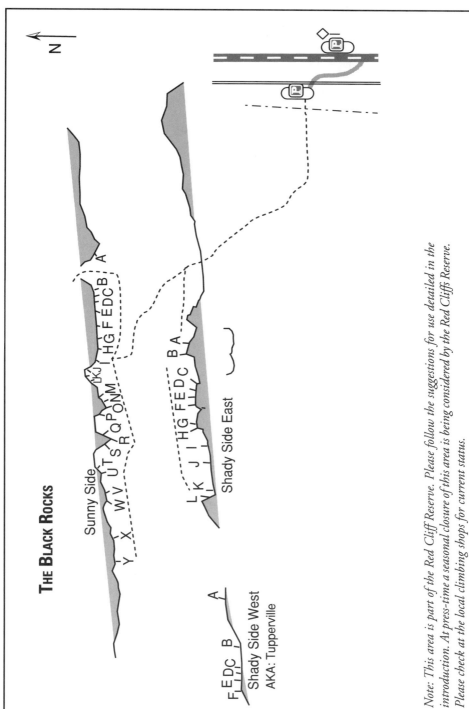

THE BLACK ROCKS

Note: *This area is part of the Red Cliff Reserve. Please follow the suggestions for use detailed in the introduction. At press-time a seasonal closure of this area is being considered by the Red Cliff Reserve. Please check at the local climbing shops for current status.*

THE BLACK ROCKS: SUNNY SIDE

A. Cyclops 5.10a*
J. Bird, T. Goss
Three bolts up edges and past eye socket to chains. (35')

B. Volcanic Therapy 5.7 TR
Use C anchor and clip directional bolt. (30')

C. Standing on Faith 5.7 TR
Two bolt anchor requires slings to set up. (35')

D. Casual Slander 5.9
D. Biniaz, E. Jones
Finger crack leads to great pockets. Three bolts to two-bolt anchor. (35')

E. Gravitational Attraction 5.11b**
T. Goss
Crimps verses gravity to pocketed overhang. Four bolts, rap hangers. (35')

F. Nuclear Decay 5.9 TR
Thin crimps on slippery face, two-bolt anchor. (35')

G. Black Hole Sun 5.8**
E. Tupper, M. Tupper
Edge past four bolts to nice pocket and open coldshuts. (35')

H. Sungrazer 5.8+**
E. Tupper, M. Tupper
Edges and pockets up a seam. Three bolts to chains. (35')

I. Black Dwarf 5.9+**
E. Tupper, M. Tupper
Blocks to reachy bulge. Four bolts to open coldshuts. (35')

J. Unknown Reality 5.9*
C. Cluff, R. Foster
Jam right hand crack in open corner. Medium gear, use K's anchors. (35')

K. Solar Eclipse 5.9***
E. Tupper, M. Tupper
Face climb between cracks in open corner. Four bolts to open shuts. (35')

L. Objective Reality 5.9***
T. Goss, A. Jones
Stem in corner through bulge to K's anchor. Small to medium gear. (35')

M. Camlock 5.10a*
W. Harding
Stem blocky corner to N's anchors. Medium gear. (40')

N. Oh My Hell 5.10c**
T. Goss
Nice face climbing on crimps and pockets. Five bolts to chains. (40')

O. Oh My Heck 5.10a***
T. Goss
Climb on the arete but clip N's bolts around the corner to right. (40')

P. Oh Shit 5.10b*
T. Goss
Flaring crack to wobbly block then up the face to rap hangers. Five bolts. (40')

Q. Jesus Wore Tevas 5.10c***
T. Goss
Stick clip first bolt of R then up and right on great crimps to chains. Four bolts. (40')

R. Moses Had A Stick Clip 5.10a***
T. Goss
A hint for the first bolt? Four bolts lead past nice edges to chains. (40')

S. Galactic Cannibalism 5.10b**
E. Tupper, M. Tupper
Nice pocket climb. Four bolts to coldshuts. (40')

T. Dark Matter 5.10c**
M. Tupper, E. Tupper
Thin and reachy crimps past 3 bolts to coldshuts. (40')

U. Degenerate Matter 5.10c**
M. Tupper, E. Tupper
Throw in a couple of shallow pockets and there you go. Three bolts to shuts. (40')

V. The Nest 5.7 TR**
Scramble up blocks to nice hold-studded face. Two-bolt anchor. (40')

W. The Keystone Arete 5.10b*
T. Goss, C. Cluff
Awkward moves around bulge, then nice moves to chains. Four bolts. (40')

X. Particulate Matter 5.11b*
M. Tupper, T. Goss
Stem up dihedral to dirty ledge, pockets to nice roof. Four bolts to chains. (40')

Y. Mickey Mantle 5.10b*
T. Goss M. Nad
Small crimps to mantle, then pockets to top. Three bolts to rap hangers. (35')

THE SHADY SIDE

A. Extinction 5.10a***

> *E. Tupper, M. Tupper*
> Climb slab and pockets past four bolts to slings. (40')

B. Polluting the Gene Pool 5.11a

> *T. Goss*
> Strange and awkward moves past four bolts to hard to clip anchors. Doesn't the name say it all? (40')

C. And God Said To Me "Stick it Dude" 5.11c*

> *FA Unknown*
> Slab to short pocketed face. Three bolts. (40')

D. Jumping to Conclusions 5.12c***

> *M. Tupper*
> Steep crimps and pockets to dyno ending. Six bolts. (45')

E. Flying off the Handle 5.12b***

> *M. Tupper*
> Shares first four bolts of D, then straight up through positive crimps to chains. Six bolts. (45')

F. Galatic Acid 5.13b**

> *M. Tupper*
> Awkward entry moves lead to a steep crimpfest. Five bolts to coldshuts. (45')

G. Slap Happy 5.12**

> *M. Nad, J. Nad*
> Slap your way up the arete past four bolts. (40')

H. Flirting With Mutants 5.11b**

> *T. Goss, M. Tupper*
> Rising left across pocketed face. Four bolts to chains. (40')

I. Ginsu 5.11c**

> *T. Goss, J. Judd*
> Difficult start leads to great moves on blunt arete. Three bolts to chains. (35')

J. Mission Impossible 5.10b**

> *D. Biniaz*
> Four bolts up positive edges convert into negative pockets. (35')
> (at press time a new route, The Beginning, was put up just right of J, four bolts to rap hangers.)

K. Entropy 5.9*

> *T. Goss*
> Short low-angled face climb on positive crimps. Good beginner lead. Four bolts, rap hangers. (35')

L. Singularity 5.10c**

> *T. Goss, E. Jones*
> Nice pockets and edges past four bolts to common anchor. (35')

M. Event Horizon 5.10d***

> *T.Goss, E. Jones*
> Wonderful arete, four bolts. (40')

N. Critical Mass 5.10c**

T. Goss

Face left of corner, nice pocket climb. Four bolts, rap hangers. (40')

O. Neutrino Drizzle 5.10b**

T. Goss

Begin right of corner up four bolts. Nice moves lead to crux at top. (40')

P. Vacuum Genesis 5.10d**

T. Goss, E. Jones

Shares first bolt with O, then up right-leaning seam passing three more bolts. (40')

THE SHADY SIDE WEST (AKA TUPPERVILLE)

A. Blank Czech 5.12a/b*

M. Nad, T. Goss

Blank is an apt description of the reachy crux. Four bolts to rap hangers. No photo. (40')

B. Escape Velocity 5.12a***

M. Tupper, E. Tupper

Sculpted rock leads to crux roof moves. Five bolts to coldshuts. (40')

C. Primeval Atmosphere 5.11b**

M. Tupper E. Tupper

Thin crimps on a sustained vertical face.
Four bolts to coldshuts. (40')

D. Primordial Soup 5.10b**

E. Tupper, M. Tupper

A natural line of face features leads to coldshuts past four bolts. (40')

E. Subdivisions 5.9**

E. Tupper, M. Tupper

Nice route for the grade shares anchors with F. Four bolts to coldshuts. (40')

F. Chromatic Aberration 5.9**

E. Tupper, M. Tupper

Edges and big pockets past three bolts to common anchor. (35')

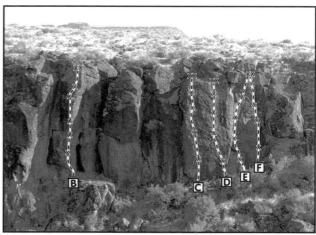

COUGAR CLIFFS

Six miles north of town on the rim of Paradise Canyon, Cougar Cliffs has always been the main "hang" for the local sport-rappeling crowd. Over the years it has apparently been necessary to check the force of gravity by tossing tires, shopping carts, dishwashers, and other miscellaneous trash into the canyon at the bottom of the cliff. Long repelled by the sight of this mess, and the plummeting bodies of local rednecks, climbers avoided this area until Ron Olevsky put up a short route on one of the varnish covered walls south of the general area of mayhem in 1993. "Pearls Before Swine" was an apt commentary on both the quality of the rock and the standards of the local misusers of it.

Drawn to more hospitable venues by the hostility of the rangers in Snow Canyon at the time, Bob Draney, Wayne Harding, and Todd Goss began development of the 120' west-facing cliff on the far south end of the formation in 1994.

The inclusion of this area into the Habitat Conservation Plan with the associated erection of a barbed wire fence has at least slowed down the litter and general degradation, as driving a vehicle to the edge of the cliff is no longer possible (stupid people are often lazy too). However, much broken glass and litter remains until a massive clean-up can be organized by the climbing community. Also, be forewarned of the potential for missing bolts and hangers on several of the routes.

Season

Anytime is pleasant in the spring and fall, summer mornings are excellent; winter afternoons this is the warmest spot on the map.

Access

Drive 6.0 miles north of Sunset Boulevard on Route 18 and turn left into a pullout just past mile marker 6.0. From the parking area, cross over the barbed wire fence and follow the dirt road downhill to a flat area east of the cliffs. Turn south and bear right of a 35' high dome with a seam in the middle (Sunday Afternoon With the Family) continue south to the top of the west-facing cliff. There is a three-bolt chain rappel anchor on a north-facing varnished step. This provides access to the bottom of the routes. A downclimb is also possible along the slabs and chimneys at the north corner of the wall. There are (or were) two fixed ropes for use as hand-lines on this descent.

Note: This area is definitely not child friendly. Sandy slabs, broken glass, plummeting rappelers, and the soft nature of the rock combine to make this area somewhat of an adventure even for grown ups.

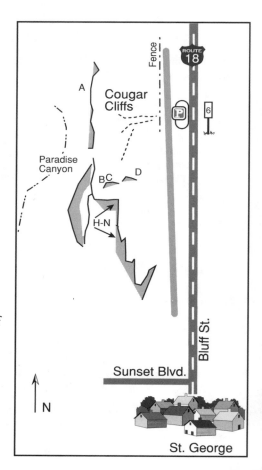

COUGAR CLIFF

A. Eat the French 5.11b*

T. Goss, C. Cluff

On a short steep face, north of the main rap area, follow three bolts up nice pockets to two-bolt anchor. Walk off. No photo shown. (30')

B. Pearls before Swine 5.9*

R. Olevsky

Ten feet right of Pigsty. Locate hard to find drilled angles, and climb jugs and pockets to a two-pin anchor. Walk off. (40')

C. Pigsty 5.9+*

T. Goss, C. Cluff

Found on the dome left of Sunday Afternoon... Climb steep varnished face on big holds. Four bolts to two-bolt anchor. Walk off. (40')

D. Sunday Afternoon with the Family 5.10a TR

W. Harding

Access the top of the dome from the south and set up a toprope from three-bolt anchor.

The following three routes are on the south facing overhanging block on the approach to the main cliff.

E. Pathetic 5.12b**

M. Tupper

Ascends the prominent overlap, requiring much in the way of body tension. Three bolts to coldshuts. Stick clip the first bolt. (35')

F. Elm Street 5.13a/b**

M. Tupper

A nightmare of thin crimps. Even harder to reach if you're shorter than Tupper. Four bolts to coldshuts. (40')

G. Cat Scratch Fever 5.11a*

T. Goss

Ascends the face on the left side of the block. Five bolts and a runout to slings. Climbing on the arete brings the grade down to 5.10c. (40')

Note: This area is part of the Red Cliffs Reserve, and is managed as habitat conservation for the desert tortoise and other threatened or endemic species. Please act responsibly when using this area, and do not allow your behavior to adversely affect the goodwill that local climbers enjoy with the area's managing agencies.

H. Project
I. Catatonic 5.10d*

> *B. Draney, S Que*
> Wandering line up pockets, past six bolts to slings. Some bolts are hard to clip. (65')

J. Delusions of Grandeur 5.11a***

> *T. Goss*
> Sustained line of beautiful sculpted pockets. Eight bolts to chains. (75')

K. Petting the Pussycat 5.10b**

> *W. Harding, T. Goss*
> Awkward entry moves lead to nice climbing up discontinuous crack system. Eight bolts to chains at 80' or continue past two more bolts to a two-bolt anchor at top, and walk off. (90')

L. Geezer Holocaust 5.11a***

> *T. Goss*
> Hard start past scary handlbar leads to great climbing above. Eight bolts to chains. (80')

M. Going for the Throat 5.11a*

> *W. Harding*
> Great moves traverse right over arch, then move left and up through some loose rock. Watch the rope drag. Eight bolts to slings. (70')

N. Indecent Exposure 5.11b**

T. Goss

From the canyon bottom climb through a scoop past nice pockets on very soft rock. Pull the overhang on varnished holds ending at slings in an alcove. Seven bolts. Toproping is very rough on rope. (75')

O. Arachnaphobia 5.10a*

T. Goss

Another very soft rock route. Delicate climbing to scoop and chains. Five bolts. (60')

Rob Foster on Indecent Exposure (5.11b)

TURTLE WALL

With the success of Chuckawalla Wall, Todd Perkins and Jorge Visser began to seek other climbing opportunities in the Paradise Canyon area north of St. George. Perkins first noticed Turtle Wall while on a training run through the canyon in November of 1994. Sitting in the open cave on the north of the formation and seeing the features on what was to become Pinching Bird Shit and Banana Dance, he felt "this simply must be bolted." Naming the area Turtle Wall for the threatened desert tortoise which inhabits this scenic but misused canyon, Visser and Perkins began developing the obvious lines in the cave which yielded some of the most unique climbing in the desert southwest. With additions by the prolific Mike and Elizabeth Tupper in 1995, Turtle Wall now sports 18 routes with grades mostly in the 5.10 through 5.12 range, and a couple of open projects which may be just a wee bit harder.

Season

Located at the bottom of Paradise Canyon with an easterly aspect, this wall is not much of a summer crag (unless 105 in the shade is what you're looking for), but at other times of the year excellent conditions prevail, with spring and fall being especially pleasant. Even on the coldest winter mornings this wall is baking in the sun, but in deep shade by afternoon.

Access

Drive 1.0 mile north of Sunset Blvd. on Bluff St. (Route 18) and pull into the pullout on the left and park. Cross the paved bike path and the fence at the step-over provided. Walk down the dirt road passing Chuckawalla Wall on the right and keep going. Take every right turn and the road will start to bear north into Paradise Canyon. Passing a grove of large cottonwood trees on the left and then a soot-covered party alcove on the right, continue north through deep sand at times and the wall will become visible on the left about 50 yards from the road. Total walking distance is about 1.0 mile or 20 minutes.

Note: This crag is part of the Red Cliffs Reserve. This area has been set aside as habitat conservation area for the desert tortoise and other threatened or endemic species. We may climb on this and other formations in this preserve as long as our activities do not affect these species. There are desert tortoises in the vicinity of this crag; if you are fortunate enough to see one you may look but don't touch. Give these animals the space and solitude that they require. Please act responsibly when using this area. Though several former party spots exist in this preserve, please do not start fires or in any other way degrade the surroundings. Do not allow your behavior to adversely affect the good will that local climbers enjoy with the agencies that manage these areas.

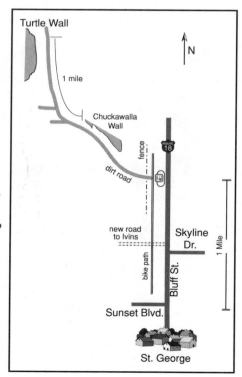

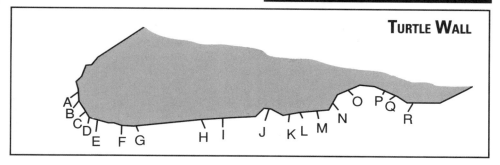

TURTLE WALL

A. Director of Humor Affairs 5.11a***
T. Perkins
The warm-up of choice: steep with big holds. Five bolts to chains. (50')

B. Lambada 5.11a**
M. Tupper, E. Tupper
Starts on the first three bolts of route A and finishes on route C's anchor with a nice traverse at the end. Four bolts. (45')

C. The Actual Parchments 5.13a***
T. Perkins
Steep and hard pocket pulling with a dyno crux to A's anchor. Seven bolts. (55')

D. Open Project

E. Open Project

F. The Waltz 5.12d**
M. Tupper, E. Tupper
A hard awkward start leads to moderate ground. Five bolts to chains. (55')

G. Tortuga 5.12a**
J. Visser, T. Perkins
Finger crack to pockets. Four bolts to chains. (55')

H. Gopherus Agassizi 5.10c
J. Visser
A three-bolt route up varnished crimps and pockets ending at chains. (40')

I. Knuckle Bones 5.10c**
E. Tupper, M. Tupper
Nice pocket route. Four bolts to coldshuts. (40')

J. Voodoo Economics 5.8**
E. Tupper, M. Tupper
A commentary on the economizing tactics of other route developers. Three bolts up pockets to coldshuts. (35')

K. Carapace 5.11a*
J. Visser
Varnished edge pulling, past four bolts to chains. (40')

L. Endangered Species 5.10d
J. Visser
Climb through large a hueco past three bolts to chains. (40')

M. Turtle Soup 5.10b
J. Visser
Another generic pocket and edge route; easier but awkward. Four bolts to chains. (40')

N. Dancing Fox 5.12b **

T. Perkins

Named for a kit fox that visited occasionally. Steep pockets past three bolts to chains on angle iron hangers. (35')

O. Pinching Bird Shit 5.11c ***

T. Perkins

Or "Pinching Bird Stuff" to some of the locals. An excellent route on great pockets climbing past four bolts to chains. (35')

P. Largado 5.12a *

J. Visser

A short steep route in the back of the cave. Three bolts to chains. (25')

Q. Banana Dance 5.11d ***

T. Perkins, J. Visser

Best route on the crag and one of the best around. Big holds and big reaches past seven bolts to chains. (40')

R. Farmers Market 5.12a *

M. Tupper

Steep pocketed route with five bolts and chains. (35')

"One of the greatest dreams of man must be to find somewhere between the extremes of nature and civilization, where it is possible to live without regret."
- Barry Lopez

BLUFF STREET CRACKS

Sitting just above Bluff street at about 500 North, a large sandstone buttress looms over the north end of town like a .... well,like a large sandstone buttress looming over the north end of town. Up here above the obligatory talus slope is some of the better crack climbing in southwestern Utah. Also evident is one of the more blatant examples of redneck stupidity in the form of some defaced pictographs.

Over the years many routes have probably been done up here, with many assents being lost to posterity (often for good reason). Herein are contained some of the better routes worth repeating.

Season
Spring, fall, and winter are prime time for this southwest facing wall with summer mornings also being tolerable.

Access
From Diagonal Street in St. George, take either 500 West or 400 West to the end of the street. Park and walk up the talus slope to the wall.

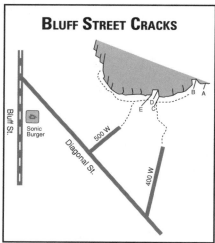

BLUFF STREET CRACKS

A. Inspired and Perspired 5.10**

G. Griscome

Obvious off-width crack splitting face to right of corner. Large pro, nothing smaller than a #3 Friend, up to #5 Camalot. (60')

B. Pig Lloyd 5.9+**

C. Cluff, C. Peterson

Nice corner crack. Small to medium pro. Rap anchor. (60')

C. Deface Crack 5.10a***

J. Visser, M. Kindred

Splitter hand crack tending to fists and knees at the top. Medium to large pro up to #4 Camalot. Chain anchor. (60')

Chris Cluff on Deface Crack (5.10a)

D. Red Warrior 5.9+**

FA Unknown

Thin corner left of A offers laybacking or thin finger jamming. Small to medium pro to #2 Camalot. Shares anchors with A. (60')

E. Wide Boy 5.10a**

FA Unknown

Hands to off-width (or layback) to hands. Medium to large pro to #4 Camalot. Two-bolt anchor. (60')

F. Freeze Dried Bat 5.10c **

B. Beck, W. Harding

Loose corner to crystal studded wall. Medium to large pro, up to #4 Camalot. Two-bolt sling anchor. No photo. (60')

GREEN VALLEY GAP

Just on the western fringe of St. George, a small canyon cuts into a rising mesa and empties into a valley better known for its mountain biking than for the rock climbing potential. But a walk up the canyon bottom reveals many short but fine walls, as well as numerous boulder problems just waiting for a chalked hand. Literally in their backyard, Todd and Chad Perkins began explorations of this scenic little canyon well before they had even heard of a carabiner, and did some "scrambles" up what are well regarded boulder problems today.

In 1994, concurrent with the general development of many sport areas around town, the Perkins pair and Casey Anderson began bolting some of the higher and harder walls, resulting in several short but enjoyable routes, and one consensus classic. Sand Stoner Reverse, which received its name by having many of its bolt holes drilled with the drill running in reverse. The route curls over the south side of the canyon like a perfect wave, and the ride is just about as smooth. This is a must do route if you are in the area.

The Gap is one of the better toproping areas in the region, and is a good area to learn the ropes for first-time climbers. A rough road runs along the top of the north side providing access to most of the anchors which are easily reached, though many require the use of slings and biners.

Season

Spring, fall, and winter are the main seasons for climbing in this, one of the lowest areas around St. George. Summer evenings can be pleasant after the sun drops behind the rim and all the south-facing climbs go into the shade.

Access

From the center of town, it is necessary to go to the west of the large basalt mesa that the airport sits on top of. This is possible either to the south or north. Either way, get on Dixie Drive Road and turn west at the sign pointing to the Green Valley Health Spa. Passing the spa on the left, continue straight to the end of the paved road past the Cottages development (passenger cars park at end of pavement). High clearance vehicles continue on gravel and turn to the right (north). Go 50 yards then turn left down a steep hill. At the bottom locate the road that runs up the mesa in front of you, and drive uphill for 0.25 miles. Turn off on spurs to the left and park. Most of the routes are on the south-facing cliff.

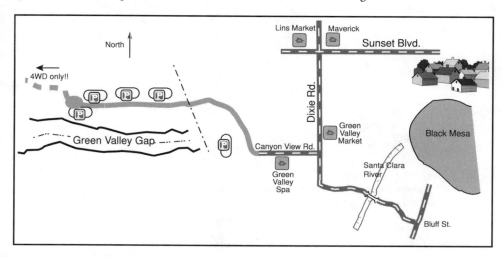

GREEN VALLEY GAP

A. Bitter Recriminations 5.10d*

T. Goss, J. Eddy

Steep start leads to nice varnished edges.
Three bolts lead to a two-bolt anchor.
Not pictured. (30')

B. 12 Gauge Conversion 5.9 TR

T. Goss

Short but fun route on edges and pockets.
Two-bolt anchor. (30')

C. Shotgun Baptism 5.10c**

T. Goss, M. Nad

Fun jump start leads to bulge finish. Four
bolts. (35')

D. Puppet Strings 5.10a**

T. Goss, M. Nad

Left side of block, up good edges to
bulge. Four bolts. (35')

E. Dueling Grandmas 5.10c

T. Goss, D. Binaz

Varnished edges and nice pockets through
four bolts to a two-bolt anchor. (35')

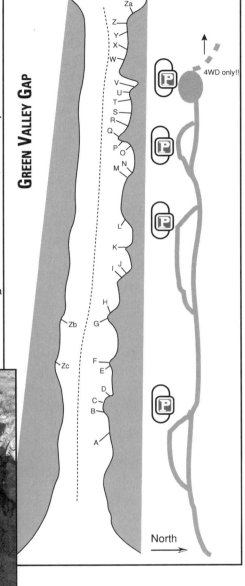

F. Fat Black Chuck 5.11b**

T. Perkins

Nice pocket climb to reachy crux. Three bolts to slings. (35')

G. Skin Graft 5.11b**

T. Perkins, C. Anderson

Beautiful arete with good varnish and long reaches. Four bolts. (35')

H. Perky's Playground 5.9**

T. Perkins

Varnish face climb past four bolts to a double-bolt anchor. (40')

I. Damned If You Do 5.8 TR

T. Goss

Short edgy toprope from a pair of bolts. (25')

J. Damned If You Don't 5.8 TR

T. Goss

Ditto.

K. The Wave 5.10b*

T. Goss

On face of pillar, nice edges to arete moves. Three bolts. (30')

L. Brazilian Ninja 5.3 TR

T. Goss

Excellent intro climb up slab. Two bolts and chains at the top. (30')

No photos for routes M-Za. Refer to overview topo.

M. The Offering 5.6 TR

T. Goss

Nice edges lead to small roof. Two-bolt anchor. (30')

N. Hairy Virgin 5.7 TR
T. Goss (Never let clients name a route!)
Crimpy start leads to slopers and small roof. Two-bolt anchor. (30')

O. The Quickening 5.12a/b**
T. Goss, D. Binaz
Steep and crimpy boulder problem. Three bolts to a two-bolt anchor. (30')

P. Moral Dilemma 5.11b***
T. Goss, T. Perkins
Steep holds on a reachy and pumpy arete lead past five bolts to a two-bolt anchor. (30')

Q. Luck 'O the Irish 5.9+**
T. Goss, J. Fitzgerald
Reachy edges and pockts leads to big holds. Three bolts to a two-bolt anchor. (30')

R. Project
S. Hair Today Gone Tomorrow 5.11d**
T. Goss, M. Nad
Smooth pockets to burly roof and bold mantle. Four bolts to chains. (35')

T. Benefit Of the Doubt 5.11a**
T. Goss, M. Nad
Reachy crimps to dubious pockets. Four bolts to a two-bolt anchor. (30')

U. Where Ego's Dare 5.9*
T. Goss, M. Nad
Three bolts worth of nice edges and varnish past big block to two-bolt anchor. (30')

V. Cool Katz 5.7*
T. Perkins, C. Katz
Good edges in stemming corner. Three bolts lead to a two-bolt anchor. (35')

W. Michael's TR 5.11d TR
M. Nad
Thin painful holds to good pockets. Two bolts at the anchor. (35')

X. Darl's Deal 5.12a TR
D. Biniaz
Weird awkward moves to more of the same. Two-bolt anchor. (35')

Y. Lambasting the Locals 5.9*
T. Goss, D. Biniaz
Hand crack to edges on varnish covered face. Four bolts to a two-bolt anchor. (35')

Z. Miscreants and Swine 5.9
T. Goss, D. Biniaz
A comment on the character of local rednecks. Four bolts through varnish edges to two-bolt anchor. (35')

Za. Scabs 5.11a TR
T. Goss
Painful edging on strange scabs of varnish. Two-bolt anchor. (35')

Zb. Short and Dorkey 5.12b*
T. Perkins
Steep!!! Nice sculpted pockets past four bolts to two-bolt anchor. (30')

Zc. Sand Stoner Reverse 5.12a***

T. Perkins, C. Anderson

Awesome climb up great holds on steep rock. Five bolts to chains. (45')

Darl Binaz on Sandstoner Reverse (5.12a)

THE POINT

Out on the end of the Green Valley Mesa, The Point provides almost guaranteed solitude with great views in every direction. While on a run along the dirt roads in his backyard, Todd Perkins discovered these southwest-facing cliffs and spent the next few weeks working with numerous friends to develop this area for climbing. Sitting on top of a short mudstone formation and necessitating delicate opening moves, this water-deposited sandstone offers a different climbing experience from anything else in the area. Deceptive pockets and apparent blank sections are passed by way of long reaches and the occasional enhanced hold. This practice is accepted by most local climbers when used to make areas with marginal climbing potential better. This area is toprope friendly with most of the anchors being two bolts on the top of the formations.

Season

All year, though in summer this is definitely an early morning or very late evening crag. In winter, spring and fall climbing is possible any time of day, with winter afternoons being superb.

Access

Complex and hard on passenger vehicles. From the end of the pavement on Canyon View road, follow gravel road to the bottom of the valley, then right along a barbed wire fence. Cross gateway in fence and follow this gravel road for 2.0 miles. Bear left at intersection and head up rough hill for 0.3 mile to parking area at the top of the crag.

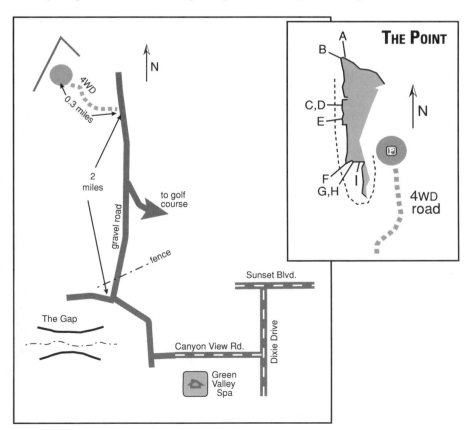

THE POINT

A. Apotheosis 5.13a***

T. Perkins, J. Visser

Fantastic arete on awesome rock. Six bolts. (65')

B. Scar Wars 5.13a**

T. Perkins, C. Perkins

Munge layer leads to gold face above, drilled pocket keeps the grade reasonable. Seven bolts to a two-bolt anchor. (65')

C. Baby Scorpion 5.12b/c**

T. Perkins, A. Holden

Shares start with D. Through edges and pockets left past six bolts. Watch out for scorpions. (55')

D. Brother Scorpion 5.12b**

T. Perkins, J. Visser

Same start; different scorpion. Four bolts. (50')

E. The Demise of Scorpio 5.12a**

T. Perkins, C. Perkins

Finally killed one! Nice route through bulge past four bolts. (50')

F. A Free Man's Choice 5.12a**

T. Perkins, A. Holden

Nice route on steep rock with varied holds. Six bolts. (50')

G. Scar Wars II 5.11b*

T. Perkins, C. Perkins

Shares start with H. Delicate munge moves lead to a fun but reachy five-bolt route. (50')

H. The Oly Strikes Back 5.11c*

T. Perkins, C. Perkins

A reference to the original route enhancer. Five bolts through pockets and nice edges. (50')

I. The Test 5.9 TR

L. Hopkinson, N. Hill

THE PROPHESY WALL

Hidden amongst the juniper covered hills north of St. George, The Prophesy Wall offers the best moderate multi-pitch climbing outside of Snow Canyon State Park. The cliffs are 200 feet high and covered with thick brown varnish on white sandstone. The location and isolation of this area provides a unique climbing experience. Long known to hikers for the maze-like labyrinth of rocks at the top of the formation, the area was developed for climbing in 1996 by Todd Goss, Ian Horn and friends, and now offers several bolted multi-pitch routes.

White sandstone tends to be less consolidated than the red variety, and the lower sections of this wall are typical of this condition. However a third of the way up the wall, the thickness of the varnish increases to the point where the rock feels like iron and offers a delightful variety of edges, pockets, and jugs to pull and stand on.

The climbing on the Prophesy Wall is typical of sandstone areas, with loose rock in abundance. While the routes have been cleaned, it is impossible to remove all the choss. The routes need to be climbed several, if not dozens, of times before much of the detritus is removed. A helmet may therefore be a good idea in an area such as this.

Season

The Prophesy Wall is another year-round area. At an elevation of 4200 feet with a west-northwest orientation it is usually 10 degrees cooler than St. George, and offers nice climbing in the mornings in the summer, and afternoons in the winter. Spring and fall are good anytime of the day.

Access

Drive north on Bluff Street out of St. George for 18.0 miles (this road turns into State Route 18). The road will climb past Snow Canyon, and several volcanic cinder cones, leaving the Mojave transitional ecosystem and enter the great basin ecosystem. At mile marker 18.0 turn left onto a gravel road (there is a brown BLM sign at the entrance to this road giving distances to Gunlock and Sand Cove Reservoirs). Follow this road for 2.0 miles past lower Sand Cove Reservoir. The wall is obvious on the left. At 2.0 miles turn left onto a dirt road and park by the big pipe. Follow the trail to the right side of the wall, and move left for other routes.

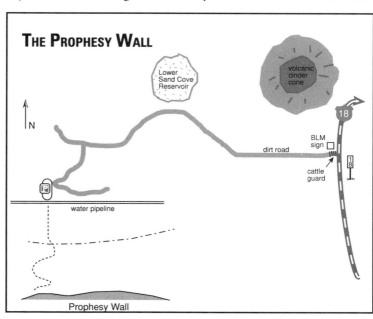

THE PROPHESY WALL

THE PROPHESY WALL

A. Seer Stone 5.3

T. Goss, A. Banard

The climb up the talus slope may be the crux of this two-bolt climb on the far east of the formation. Chain anchor. (35')

B. Softscrub 5.7 TR

I. Horn

Soft sandstone slopers and brittle varnish. Sandy ledges provide access to the two-bolt anchor. (45')

C. Elizabeth Blue Moss 5.9*

T. Goss

Never let a client name a route. Pockets and varnish to moss finish. Five bolts and chains. (55')

D. The Roofs of Jericho 5.10c***

I. Horn, T. Goss

1st Pitch: Begin right of a dihedral and, climb excellent varnished edges past nine bolts. It is possible to end before the crux roof by stepping left to anchors below the arch (5.9). The pitch normally pulls the roof to a belay on top of the arch. (95', 5.10c)

2nd Pitch: From the arch pull edges to a small roof and chains at 65'.

Descent: Rap the route with two ropes or walk off Southeast.

E. Project
F. Project

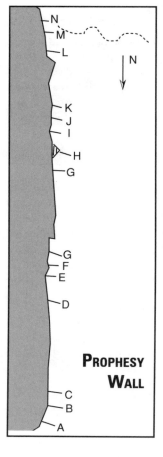

PROPHESY WALL

G. Grumpy Old Men 5.10b**

T. Goss, D. Binaz

1st Pitch: Climb up spine of delicate flakes jutting out from crack then head up reachy slopers past ten bolts to anchor. (110')

2nd Pitch: Move through roof on soft holds then bomber varnish to chains. Nine bolts. (90')

Descent: Rap Misfit Prophets with one rope.

H. Misfit Prophets 5.10c**

T. Goss, B. Beck

1st Pitch: From the ledge at the foot of Jabba the Hut (rock formation shaped like the **Star Wars** character), climb sandy slopers then up steep varnish and pockets past eleven bolts to anchor. (5.10c, 80')

2nd Pitch: Steep varnish and jugs past nine bolts leads to two-bolt anchor on a ledge with big tree. (5.9, 80')

3rd Pitch: Iron hard varnish and huge holds. Five bolts. (5.8, 60')

Descent: Rap the route with one rope or walk off in either direction

I. Lunatic Cry 5.10**

T. Anderson

1st Pitch: Begins 20' right of route H, and climbs a finger and hand crack to a single bolt and gear anchor. (5.9+, 80')

2nd Pitch: Crack in dihedral to overhung hands, then up a ramp to a three-bolt anchor. (5.10, 80')

3rd Pitch: Traverse 20' left across a ledge to an easy splitter to the top. (5.7)

Descent: Rap route H.

J. Project

K. Project

L. Caging the Zealot 5.10b***

T. Goss, E. Jones

1st Pitch: Angle up a ramp then up steep varnish past fifteen bolts to the ledge with a tree and chains. (5.10b, 145')

2nd Pitch: Varnished jugs lead past four bolts to chains. (5.8, 50')

Descent: Three single rope rappels.

M. The Visionaries 5.10c***

T. Goss, I. Horn, T. Broderick

1st Pitch: Edges and pockets lead up ever steepening wall past 13 bolts, ending at chains on the ledge with a tree. (5.9+, 145')

2nd Pitch: Short finger crack to varnish edges. Three bolts to chains. (5.10c, 50')

Descent: Rap the route with one rope. Three raps.

N. Sticky Revelations 5.10a***

T. Goss, I. Horn

1st Pitch: Big varnished edges lead past eight bolts to chains on ledge. (5.7, 70')

2nd Pitch: Nice edges lead to rising left traverse. Eight bolts. (5.8, 75')

3rd Pitch: Delicate flake and edges past four bolts to chains. (5.10a, 45')

Descent: Rap the route with one rope. Three rappels.

Variations

1. Exodus Variation 5.3

Follow ledges left past four bolts to M's anchor. (40')

2. Variation to 2nd Pitch of N 5.8***

M. Nad, J. Nad

At the top of the 1st pitch of route N, traverse left on big ledge to corner. Jam up beautiful varnished crack to 2nd pitch anchors on N. Small to medium pro. (40')

"God grant me the serenity to accept the things I cannot change, the courage to change the things I can, and wisdom to know the difference."
- Reinhold Niebuhr

PIONEER PARK

Pioneer Park, born out of the locals' need for a training ground, started as a single traverse discovered by Jorge Visser. Once the loose outer layers of stone broke away, and pockets were cleaned out this traverse became the focal point for this dedicated crew every evening. The *de facto* chairman, for this board of boulderers, was Wade Widdeson, who relentlessly pursued every conceivable problem and eliminate as well as discovering and developing numerous new walls. The area now has a myriad of developed walls providing bouldering from easy to hard. Landings are generally good but a crash pad would not be a bad idea on some problems.

Listing all of the established problems would require a book in itself, and most climbers casually traverse or make up problems for one another. Due to the casual nature of both the problems (and the locals) no V grades have been recorded or presented in this book. If you happen to run into locals, they may be a great source of information or perhaps even encouragement.

To prevent this fragile rock from breaking, please wait about 24 hours after a rainstorm before climbing. This area is also the habitat of *Redneckus Americanus*, the normal behavior of which is to throw beer bottles at the rocks. Watch for glass in the pockets in some locations.

Season
Year round area offering sun or shade as desired. Spring and Summer evenings can be buggy as there is a spring not far away.

Access
Take 1000 E. north of St. George Blvd, and turn left onto Skyline Dr. for 0.5 mile. After passing the water tanks on the left, turn right onto Pioneer Park Loop Road, and park by the second covered picnic table. The park is open from sunrise to sunset.

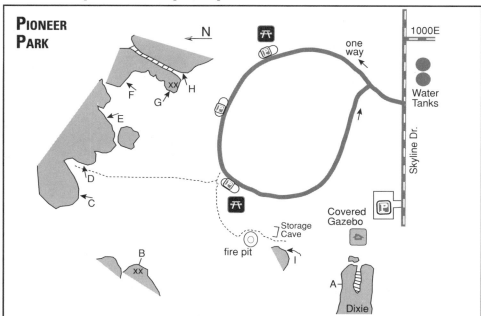

PIONEER PARK

A. Dixie Cave
A large cave behind the rock with "Dixie" painted on it yields traversing and overhanging buckets. This is unfortunately a big party spot so watch out for glass.

B. Child's Play 5.8 TR
A short slabby toprope with a three-bolt anchor.

C. Toe Hook Traverse
The wall to the left of the Main Traverse offers some rather esoteric moves through the crux.

D. The Main Traverse
Recognizable by the amount of chalk, this brilliant formation offers almost unlimited problems and eliminates.

E. Cut Finger Traverse
Sun in the morning and shade in the afternoon. This formation has somewhat worse landings and slightly different textured rock than the other problems here.

F. Bird Nest Traverse
A nice but committing problem with a slightly loose finish.

G. Choss Tower 5.9 TR
Two bolts on top should be backed up with the slung pillar. Nice pocket climbing.

H. The Narrows Traverse
A small slot canyon has some chalked holds on the right.

I. The Corncob Boulder
Steep and powerful moves with several problems completed.

"The reasonable man adapts himself to the world; the unreasonable man persists in trying to adapt the world to himself. Therefore all progress depends on the unreasonable man."
- George Bernard Shaw

SNOW CANYON STATE PARK

Darl Biniaz on Passion (5.11d)

SNOW CANYON STATE PARK

Around the mid-70's, with technical climbing approaching its golden age in Yosemite, local climbers began to explore the potential of the large sandstone walls of Snow Canyon. Mike Anderson, Matt Kindred, Ron Olevsky, and John Tainio explored face routes on this delicate desert varnish as well as the alluring crack climbs.

Snow Canyon is probably the only area in southwestern Utah that experienced the ethical wars of the late 80's and early 90's. The rap bolting of several sport climbs in the canyon challenged a staunch ground-up ethic. Though no bolts were chopped, complaints and arguments attracted the attention of the rangers for the first time. When one individual created several routes by drilling finger pockets in the soft sandstone, events eventually came to a head with pockets filled in with grout by angered climbers and the first ascentionist re-drilling them several times. With rising complaints from climbers about each other and obvious resource degradation, the park imposed a moratorium on the installation of new bolts in 1994.

In 1998 a resource management plan was approved for Snow Canyon State Park. This plan is the culmination of almost four years of effort by many people, including local climbers who fought continually for the privilege to climb and develop new routes in the park. As part of the new management plan, a climbing advisory team processes new route applications and makes recommendations to the park manager who is the approving authority.

To Maintain our good relations with the park managers please:
1. Be considerate to other users of the park, pick up your trash.
2. Use the established approaches and belay areas.
3. Pay the $4.00 per vehicle day-use fee. There is prevalent ticketing of offenders.
4. Toilets are located at the campground and at the West Canyon parking area. Please use them. Turds don't decompose in the desert.

Season
Take Bluff St. 0.75 mile north of the Sunset Blvd. intersection to the Snow Canyon Parkway. Turn left onto the parkway and drive 6.0 miles to the intersection of Utah Route 8. Turn right and drive 3.0 miles into Snow Canyon State Park.

Access
The single biggest impact that we as climbers have on the park is the impact generated getting to and from the climbs. Please follow the directions in the center map for parking and approach each climbing area by the directions given. The park has approved these approaches, and deviations from them will jeopardize our continued access to many of these areas.

Should you find yourself off route on the approach, consider the following:
- Walk on a durable surface (sand or sandstone), and avoid stepping on fragile moss or lichens which sometime grow on the rock surface.
- Washes are the areas of greatest biodiversity, and harbor plant and animal life uncommon to other areas of the park. Step lightly and stay on sand or rock if possible.
- Avoid walking on Cryptobiotic (Microbiological) soil. It is the dark crust that holds the surface layer together and prevents erosion and takes centuries to recover.
- Avoid walking beneath obvious nesting sites for birds or raptor species.

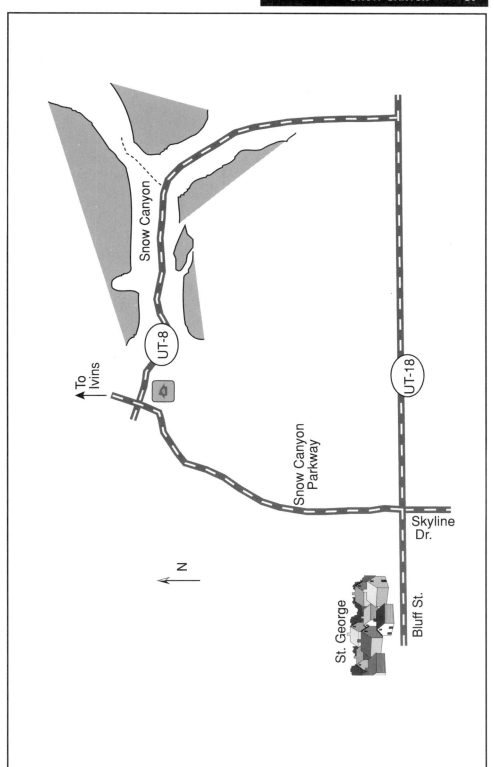

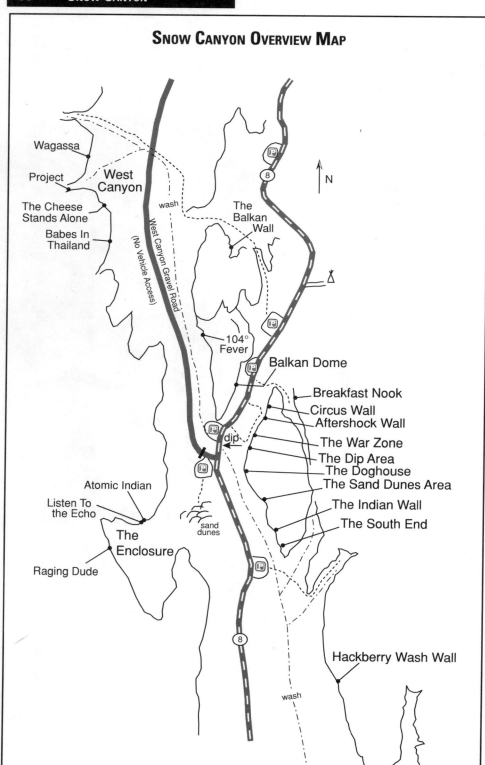

SNOW CANYON OVERVIEW MAP

Wagassa

Project

West Canyon

The Cheese Stands Alone

Babes In Thailand

wash

West Canyon Gravel Road

(No Vehicle Access)

The Balkan Wall

N

104° Fever

Balkan Dome

Breakfast Nook
Circus Wall
Aftershock Wall

The War Zone
The Dip Area
The Doghouse
The Sand Dunes Area

dip

The Indian Wall

The South End

Atomic Indian

Listen To the Echo

The Enclosure

Raging Dude

sand dunes

8

Hackberry Wash Wall

wash

8

HACKBERRY WASH

Access

Park at the pullout for Jenny's Canyon. Follow signed trail to wash. Turn south and follow wash for 0.12 mile to a cryptic trail leading up to the wall.

A. Deviant Chimney 5.4*

M. Kindred
Between a standing block and wall. Three bolts in chimney to sling anchor. (35')

B. Pillar of Faith 5.10b**

T. Goss, A. Jones
Wide and awkward crack to thin varnish face. Four bolts and medium pro to sling anchor. (70')

C. Who Knows What It's Called 5.11a***

FA: Unknown
Thin varnish face climbing on delicate features. Eleven bolts to chains. (75')

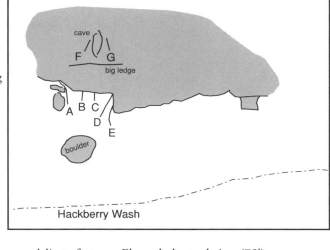

D. Deviated Septum 5.10c**

J. Tainio
Crack in left corner, hands to fists at top. Medium to large pro. Chain anchor. (70')

E. Project

F. Pygmy Brain 5.9

L. Bjornson, J. Tainio
This adventure climbs a slabby face to left of cave. Small to medium pro and four bolts. Use pro for anchor. (40')

G. The Right Stuff 5.10

J. Tainio, L. Bjornson
Low angle friction face to right of cave. Five pins and bolts to a two-bolt anchor; medium pro helpful. (40')

ISLAND IN THE SKY - SOUTH END

Access

Park at the pullout for Jenny's Canyon trail at mile marker 9. Follow signed trail to the southern tip of Island In the Sky.

A. Another Roadside Attraction 5.9*

J. Tainio, L. Bjornson, M. Kindred

1st Pitch: Friction slab past two bolts to flake, up and left past two more bolts to pit with chain anchor. Small pro. (5.9, 80')

2nd Pitch: Out pit to right past one bolt to higher pit. Rap chains way out left. Two raps to the ground. This pitch isn't worth the trouble. (5.9, 30')

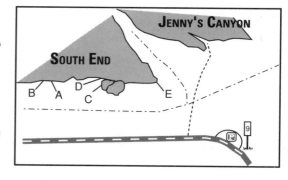

B. Main Attraction Variation 5.10c*

M. Anderson, M. Kindred

Three bolt variation to start of A.

C. Confused Groundhog 5.10a TR

J. Visser, M. Kindred

Varnish edges and pockets on block to right of chimney. Sling block at top for anchor. (40')

D. DOA 5.9 X

J. Tainio

1st pitch: At top of chimney make unprotected traverse to first bolt (X rated) then past four bolts to slings in middle of wall. (5.9, 40')

2nd Pitch: Friction slab traverse past three bolts to slings. (5.9, 70' rap to ground)

E. Jimmy Durante 5.9* R

M. Kindred J. Visser, M. Anderson

1st Pitch: Friction slab through overlap. Four bolts to chains. Medium pro. (5.9, 60')

2nd Pitch: Friction on slopers and Moki marbles past four bolts to chains. (5.8, 90')

3rd Pitch: 4th class to ledge. (70')

Descent: Walk off north, down scree slope.

ISLAND IN THE SKY - THE INDIAN WALL

Access
Park at the pullout for Jenny's Canyon trail at mile marker 9.0. Follow signed trail to the wash and then head up the wash for 50 yards to a cryptic trail leading up to the wall.

A. Raindance 5.10a** R
> *M. Anderson, M. Kindred*
> Begin in a scrub oak tree, friction past six bolts and a cam placement in a flake to chains. (85' — watch you don't rap off the end of your rope!!!).

B. Pierced Ear 5.10c**
> *S. Unice, J. Christenson*
> Steep slab past twelve bolts to anchor in alcove. Rap with two ropes or walk off north. (100')

C. Tomahawk 5.10c*
> *M. Kindred, M. Anderson*
> **1st Pitch:** Friction slab past four bolts to chain anchor in pit. (5.8, 40') 7 I/o w/ Sparky
> **2nd Pitch:** Traverse out of pit to left past one bolt to route B. (5.10c, 60')

D. Kindred Spirits 5.7* R   7/10 TR w/ Spenser
> *M. Anderson, M. Kindred*
> The first bolt is way the hell up there. Friction up the slab past two more bolts. Leads to chains in a pit. (50')
> Variation: Staying left seems slightly harder.

E. Handful of Crack Fistful of Pockets 5.9**   7/10 w/ Spenser
> *J. Visser M. Kindred*
> **1st Pitch:** Flake and varnish face to sling anchor. Medium to large pro. (5.7, 40')
> **2nd Pitch:** Steep pockets past two bolts to two-bolt anchor. (5.9, 30')
> Decent: Walk off north then down scree slope.

Jesse Lee on Clairvoyance (5.11b)

ISLAND IN THE SKY - SAND DUNES AREA

Access

Park at the West Canyon day use parking lot. Walk south on paved road for 100 yards. Head east across wash to obvious scree slope for access to second tier.

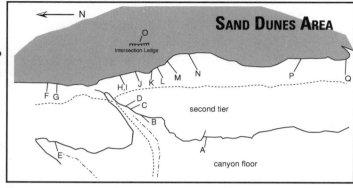

A. Rat Race 5.9*

J. Visser, M. Kindred

1st Pitch: Left side of arch, climb wide crack, traverse right to two-bolt anchor at apex of arch. Medium to large pro. (5.9, 70')

2nd Pitch: Slopey slab past three bolts to gear anchor. Walk off north then down scree slope. (5.9)

B. Nemesis 5.10d**

L. Bjornson, J. Tainio

Friction slab to a committing mantle and thin varnish face climbing. #3 TCU helpful towards the top. Sling anchor. Rap the route. (80')

C. Little Miss Demeanor 5.10a

R. Olevsky

1st Pitch: Natural pockets to drilled finger pockets through blank section. Seven pins to a two-pin anchor with no slings. (5.10a, 65')

2nd Pitch: Traverse left past two pins to two-pin anchor above route D. (5.9, 30')

Descent: Walk off north and down scree slope.

D. Twist and Shout 5.7*

R. Olevsky

Slab and horizontal cracks past four pins to a two-pin anchor. Medium gear for runout section. Walk off north. (70')

E. Clairvoyance 5.11b***

J. Visser

Slopey pockets, to overhanging scoop, finish on thin varnish edges to the top. Twelve bolts to two-bolt anchor. (95')

Descent: Walk off south. Mid-station anchor allows toprope of lower half .

F. Kibosch Buttress 5.6*

R. Olevsky

Ramp and varnish slab past seven pins to chains. Medium gear useful. Two raps to ground. (90')

G. Kibosch 5.11b

R. Olevsky

1st Pitch: Short friction slab to chains in pocket. Two pins. (5.8, 40')

2nd Pitch: Out right past seven pins on thin varnish and two drilled pockets to the triple pin anchor above chains on route F. (5.11b, 70')

3rd Pitch: Traverse left to base of crack, then up to chain anchor. Medium to large gear. (5.9, 60')

Descent: Rap the route, or walk off east and scramble down ledges (serious 4th class!).

Anthony Jones on Leopard Skin (5.7)

"Sceptical scrutiny is the means, in both science and religon, by which deep thoughts can be winnowed from deep nonsense"
- Carl Sagan

H. A Little Nightmare Music 5.8*

R. Olevsky

Hand crack on right side of huge boulder (medium gear). Scary block in middle (you may hear nightmare music). Anchor slings, rap the route. (60')

I. Full Metal Jockstrap 5.9** R

R. Olevsky

1st Pitch: Begins at top of route H. Traverse left past four pins to two-pin anchor. (5.8, 35')

2nd Pitch: Thin varnish past eight pins (runout) to two-pin anchor. (5.9, 80')

3rd Pitch: Friction slab to big ledge, traverse to top. (60')

Descent: Walk off south to Wills Rush rappel. Four raps to the ground.

J. Will's Rush 5.5*

S. Jensen, L. Jessup

On a historical note, this was the first route in Snow Canyon.

1st Pitch: Up prominant ramp past trees and bushes for pro to flat ledge with two-pin anchor. Medium gear. With a 50m rope either simul-climb or belay at alcove. (5.5, 180')

2nd Pitch: Friction face to right of chimney (four pins) pass mid-station to chains. (95')

Descent: Rap to ledge, then down route M to ground.

K. Extra Texture 5.7* R

R. Olvesky

From base of route L begin rising left traverse past five pins to chains left of cave. (70') Rap the route.

L. Stepping Out 5.9**

R. Olevsky

1st Pitch: Thin crack to chains. Small to medium gear. (5.9, 50')

2nd Pitch: Friction slab past five pins to chains. (5.8, 50')

3rd Pitch: Slopers past six pins to chains just below big ledge. (5.8, 60')

4th Pitch: One pin to intersection ledge with two-pin anchor. Access chimney to south of ledge and make three raps to the ground.

Note: Not all pins are depicted on the photo. Also, this route is much more enjoyable if the 2nd, 3rd, and 4th pitches are combined. 50m rope OK.

M. Battle of Wills 5.9

R. Olevsky

Loose dirty chimney, best used as a descent route.

N. Prestidigitator 5.10a

R. Olevsky

1st Pitch: Sloper edges past four pins to two-pin anchor. (5.9, 50')

2nd Pitch: Friction right to access flake, chipped for fingers with small to medium gear to chains. (5.10a, 50')

3rd Pitch: Traverse right, then left past six pins to chains. (5.9, 60')

4th Pitch: Varnish face and crack to chains on route O. (5.7, 65')

5th Pitch: Varnish slab past two pins and cracks to top. Gear for anchor.

Descent: Walk south and rap route J to ledge, then M.

O. A Thousand Pints of Lite 5.7**

R. Olevsky

1st Pitch: From intersection ledge walk east to chimney, then traverse right past one pin to three-pin anchor above just above ledge. (5.1, 50')

2nd Pitch: Varnish acmes past two pins to chains. (5.7, 50')

3rd Pitch: Huge varnish jugs past six pins to two-pin anchor. (5.7, 80')

Descent: Walk north to route J, rap it, then route M to ground.

P. Leopard Skin 5.7**

R. Olevsky

1st Pitch: Friction slab past two pins to crack (medium gear). One-pin anchor with #1 camalot. (5.7, 50')

2nd Pitch: Right traverse past four pins and up to two-pin anchor. (5.7, 65')

3rd Pitch: Varnish slab past seven pins to three-pin anchor. (5.6, 70')

4th Pitch: Varnish acmes past seven pins to slings. (5.6, 70')

Descent: Walk off south, rap chimney to Q and rap to ground.

Q. Stranger Than Friction 5.8*

R. Olevsky

Friction slab and steps past five pins to chains. (70')

ISLAND IN THE SKY - THE DOGHOUSE

Access

Park in the West Canyon day use lot. Walk across the street, across the wash, and up the sandstone slab into The Doghouse.

A. Dogma 5.12b**

T. Goss, D. Biniaz

Huecos to slopers past four bolts to rap anchors. (35')

B. Dogface 5.11d*

M. Nad, J. Nad

Pockets and edges up steep wall past six bolts to sling anchor on C. (60')

C. The Doghouse Arete 5.11b***

J. Visser

Blunt arete on pockets, and varnish edges. Five bolts to sling anchor on ledge. (50')

D. Meaty Bone 5.12b***

J. Visser

Ever shrinking pockets and edges up ever steepening face. Seven bolts to chains. (70')

E. All Bark and No Bite 5.11d**

J. Nad, M. Nad

Varnish pockets and crimps past six bolts to chain anchor. (60')

F. Project

G. Just Another Crack 5.10c*

J. Visser, M. Kindred

Wide crack in corner Large pro required. Walk off north. (60')

H. Just Another Chimney 5.6

M. Kindred

Chimney in right corner of alcove, medium to large pro. Walk off north. (60')

I. Hair of the Dog 5.10b**

B. Beck, T. Goss

Route starts in chimney and traverses onto face. Seven bolts to rap anchor. (60')

Rob Foster on The Doghouse Arete (5.11b)

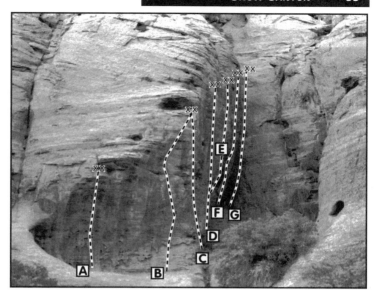

ISLAND IN THE SKY - DIP AREA

Access

Just after the dip there is a pullout on the left. Park here and walk across the road and north 100' to a trail which leads to an arch. Route is around the corner to the left.

A. Under the Sleeping Giant 5.6**

J. Tainio, M. Kindred

Huge leaning block against a slab, between arch and moss covered wall. Climb crack and face in corner. Small to large pro needed. Anchor bolts missing hangers. Walk off south and then down slabs to 4th class dihedral. (This route is in the shade all day).

ISLAND IN THE SKY - THE WAR ZONE

Note: The first three routes in this area have drilled finger pockets, and altered or created edges that were manufactured by the first ascentionist. Some of them have been filled in, others remain as is. The RMP mandates no chipping, drilling, gluing, or manufacturing of holds. This means that these routes will remain in "as is" condition, and no further tactics of this nature will be tolerated in the Park.

Access

Park in the pullout just after the dip in the road on the left. Walk north 100' to signed trail. Follow trail for 100 yards to obvious black varnished wall.

A. The Fray 5.11d

R. Olevsky

Vertical black varnish wall. Hard start to drilled finger pockets past four pins to chains. The first bolt is ridiculously high. (45')

B. Black Massacre 5.11b

R. Olevsky

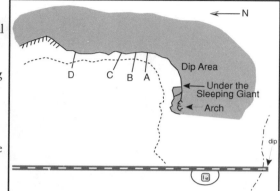

1st Pitch: Bouldery start to several drilled finger pockets past six pins to chains. (5.11b, 60')

2nd Pitch: Steep varnish climbing on crimps and incut edges. One drilled finger pocket just before chains. Six pins. (5.10c, 65')

3rd Pitch: Traverse out left then rising right hand traverse past nine pins to chains (hard to see the anchor from the last pin).

Note: This route goes at 5.11d without any of the drilled holds.

C. Dr. Yes 5.10d

R. Olevsky

Bouldery start past six pins to chains. A medium cam is useful in runout section. (60')

Note: The route is 5.11a without any of the drilled holds

D. The Richness Of It All 5.12a***

D. Biniaz, T. Goss

Four pitches to the right of prominate long alcove. Access via Pioneer names trail.

1st pitch: Crimps and pockets up ever steepening wall to rap anchor. Nine bolts. (5.11a, 80')

2nd pitch: Leftward rising traverse up relentless wall of crimpy edges. Eleven bolts to rap anchor on small ledge. (5.12a, 80')

3rd pitch: Leftward rising traverse through beautiful sculpted features, pull small roof and then move right to rap anchor on ledge. Twelve bolts. (5.11c, 80')

4th pitch: Climb fantastic twisting arete past twelve bolts to rap anchor at peak of arete. (5.11c, 90')

Descent: Rap the route via four rappels to the ground.

Note: 60 meter rope is recommended for this route.

"There is no limit to the good a man can do if he doesn't care who gets the credit."
- *unknown*

ISLAND IN THE SKY - AFTERSHOCK WALL

Access

Park in the pullout on the left after the dip. Walk 100' north on the road to signed trail. Follow rock lined trail 150 yards to wall atop slickrock ledges. This wall is 30 feet to the right of the Circus Wall.

A. Aftershock 5.11b***

J. Visser, B. Beck, W. Harding

1st Pitch: Friction slab traverse past two-bolts to base of flake, climb past one pin and medium stopper placement to chains atop flake. (5.10a, 60')

2nd Pitch: Rising right traverse on thin varnish edges past eight bolts to chain anchor in cave. (5.10c, 80')

3rd Pitch: Out of cave to the left, through overhang and onto varnished slab. Six bolts to sling anchor in alcove. (5.10c, 65')

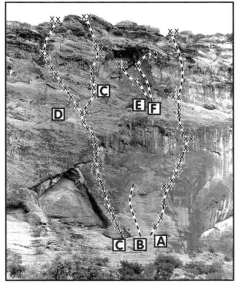

4th Pitch: Traverse right into overhanging finger crack to top of formation. Small to medium pro. Walk off North and down ledges on north tip of formation. (5.11b, 65') From top of 3rd pitch possible to rap to the ground with single rope via mid-station beneath cave.

Note: Not all bolts are shown on photo.

B. Project

Five pins to nowhere.

C. Living on the Edge 5.10c***

W. Harding and friends

1st Pitch: Rising left traverse along edge of alcove past eight bolts to chains. (5.10a, 60')

2nd Pitch: Sketchy choss leads to overhang and rising left traverse past ten bolts to sling anchor on big ledge. (5.10c, 80')

3rd Pitch: Right and up off of ledge gains slab leading to thin detached flake, mantle and climb more slab to slings in alcove. Six bolts. (5.10c, 70')

4th Pitch: One bolt gains an awkward crack. Small to medium gear. (5.9, 70')

Descent: Walk off north and down ledges at north tip of formation or rap back down the route (anchors on top hard to find).

Note: Not all bolts shown on photo.

D. Quisquose 5.10a

W. Harding, R. Judd

From anchor on big ledge move up left past seven traversing bolts to thin crack and anchor. Short second pitch to the top. Small to large pro. Walk off. (70')

E. Zee Traverse 5.8

W. Harding, A. Brooking

Traverse along ledge and set gear anchor beneath overhang. Climb crack past a lone bolt to sling anchor and rap back down to ledge. Small to large pro. (60')

F. Women in Lycra 5.10b

W. Harding

Same approach as for E. Up crack to bolt and hand traverse to anchor. Rap back to ledge. (50')

ISLAND IN THE SKY - THE CIRCUS WALL

Access

Park at the Hidden Pinon Trailhead and walk 200 yards south on road to Pioneer Names Trail. Follow rock-lined trail to wall.

Note: A bristling forest of drilled angles litters this wall. The drilled angles as well as several routes are not described for the sake of clarity.

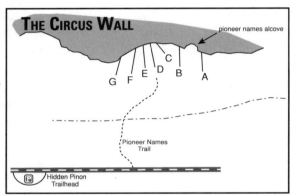

A. Trapeze 5.10b

R. Olevsky

Two pitches of rope drag on thin varnish. Not worth the effort.

B. Roar of the Greasepaint 5.10a***

R. Olevsky

1st Pitch: Thin and slopey varnish traversing to the right past eight pins to chains. (5.10a, 70')

2nd Pitch: Up and left on big holds past four pins to chains. (5.9, 60')

Note: A variation moves up and right through slightly harder terrain following four pins.

C. Illegal Alien 5.10b**

R. Olevsky

Friction slab to vertical varnished face. Ten pins lead to anchors in pit. Runout to first pin can be bypassed by way of climbing the first two pins of route D then traversing right. The eyes of pins on this route are painted red. (140')

D. Pygmy Alien 5.7***

R. Olevsky

1st Pitch: Friction slab to varnish edges past twelve pins to anchors in pit. The eyes of pins are painted green. (5.7, 140')

2nd Pitch: Left out of the pit, passing three pins to gain hand and finger crack leading to the top of the formation. Small to large pro. (5.7, 100')

Descent: Walk off north, then down ledges at north tip of formation.

E. Freak Show 5.9

R. Olevsky

Nine pins wandering all over the wall to anchors in pit. (140')

F. Jimmy the Geek 5.9**

R. Olevsky

1st Pitch: Friction slab past five blue pins and short crack to three-pin anchor. Small to medium pro. (5.9, 90')

2nd Pitch: Steep scoop on varnish edges past three pins to anchor in pit. (5.9, 50')

G. The Barbarian 5.6**

R. Olevsky, K. Stephens

1st Pitch: Friction slab past two pins, to right facing corner. Varnish acmes to slings on ledge. Medium to large pro. (100')

2nd Pitch: Runout on acmes past two pins to hand crack in corner. Medium to large pro to tree, and gear belay.

4th class to the top.

Descent: Walk off north and down ledges.

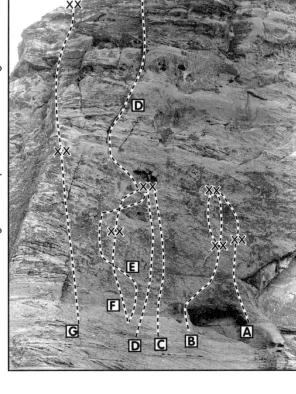

THE BREAKFAST NOOK

Access

Park at Hidden Pinon Trailhead. Walk 100 yards south on paved road to signed trail. Routes are 100 yards up the trail on the left.

A. The Colliewobbles 5.10a**

T. Goss, B. Beck

Wonderful pockets and varnish edges past seven bolts to rap anchor. (70')

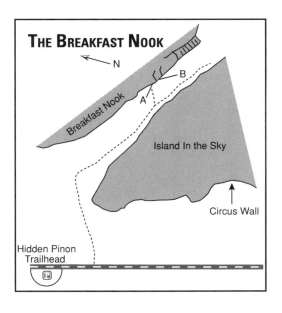

B. Bat's Meow 5.7**

M. Anderson, M. Kindred

Varnish acme climbing with discontinuous cracks for pro. Medium to large gear. (85')

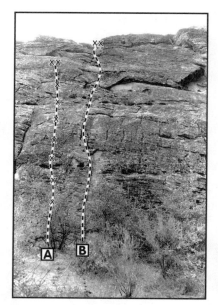

BALKAN DOME

Access

Park in pullout on left after the dip in the road. Take trail west to wash for 50 yards. Turn right on trail which runs along crag for 100 yards.

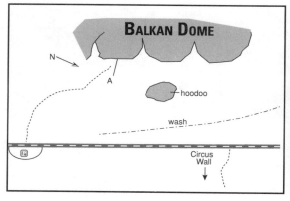

A. Ledinski Declines 5.8*

R. Olevsky

Route is atop slickrock ledges across the street from the Aftershock Wall. Friction face and slopers past five pins to two-pin anchor. (65')

Descent: Walk off south, and downclimb chimney in alcove.

B. 104 Fever 5.11d**

R. Olevsky

Approach

Park at pullout after dip in road on the left. Follow trail west into wash for 400 yards to overhanging streaked wall atop a pedestal on the right. Route is in the middle of the wall.

Overhanging huecos and varnish edges past fourteen pins to gear anchor. No topo shown. (90')

BALKAN WALL

Access

Park at Hidden Pinon Trailhead and follow Hidden Pinon Trail past display post #10. Just after the trail goes under some stacked boulders locate the trail in a wash to the left. Follow the wash to this obvious east-facing wall.

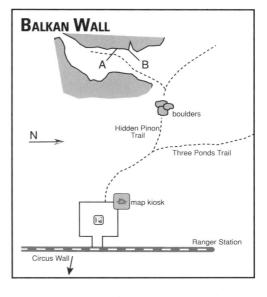

A. Goryenko's Triumph 5.10b**

R. Olevsky

Vertical face on varnish edges past seven pins to crack (medium pro) to chains in alcove. (60')

B. The Waiting Game 5.11c TR

FA Unknown

Beautiful sharp arete, with varnish crimpers at top. Access chains on top from north on slickrock.

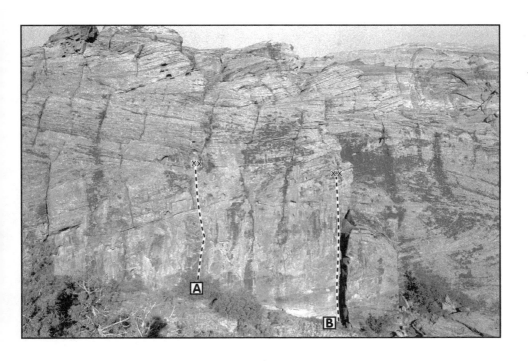

THE ENCLOSURE

Access

Park at West Canyon day use lot. Follow hiking/bike path south to the wash. Follow wash into Enclosure Canyon.

A. Atomic Indian 5.11***

FA. Unknown
Overhanging hand to finger crack. 60' to pin/stopper/bolt anchor. Medium to large pro.

7/01
w/Spencer
B. Uncle Reamus 5.8**

J. Tainio, M. Kindred
Steep edging on hollow sounding slopers past two bolts to handcrack. Sling anchor after Medium pro. (60')

C. Malice in Gobi Land 5.11 A2 or 3?

J. Tainio
Aid seam to finger crack. Sling anchor at 50'. Handcrack to top. Aid pro unknown. Free pro: small to medium gear. Walk off north.

D. Listen to the Echo 5.10a** Spencer 7/10

J. Visser, M. Kindred
Pure friction past five bolts, and bold mantle to sling anchor. (60')

scares

E. Don't Fear the Reamer 5.10a**

J. Tainio, J. Visser

Corner crack and flake system up nice hand crack to sling anchor. (80')

Access

Follow wash west to far northwest corner of the Enclosure Canyon. Wall faces east.

F. Raging Dude 5.11a**

C. Pendleton, G. Olsen

Huecos and sloper edges to arch then, bad pockets to slings. Five bolts and pins, though at press time the second to last bolt had been stolen.

G. Grinder 5.9*

J. Visser, M. Kindred

Wide start leads to nice hand crack in sharp corner. Medium to large pro. Use F's anchor.

West Canyon

Access

Park at West Canyon Day Use Area and follow gravel road north for approximately 0.75 miles.

Note: Inquire at the ranger station concerning closures for nesting raptors prior to attempting this climb.

A. Babes in Thailand 5.10a*

R. Olevsky, M Pey

1st Pitch: Friction slab with crack to two-pin anchor. (5.6)
2nd Pitch: Runout friction face to two-pin anchor. (5.4)
3rd Pitch: Friction slab past three bolts to two-pin anchor at base of ramp. (5.5)
4th Pitch: Scramble up ramp to ledge. Two-pin anchor. (5.6)
5th Pitch: Stem and clamber up chimney past bulge to two-pin belay. (5.9)
6th Pitch: Up dihedral to gear belay. (5.8)
7th Pitch: Face past two bolts to corner crack. (5.6)
8th Pitch: Right then up mossy slab to two-pin anchor. (5.8)
9th Pitch: Crack to pin, pull roof crack to a belay. (5.10a)
10th Pitch: Friction slab to the top. (5.6)

Pro: Bring a full rack, and possibly some extra webbing to replace some of the old stuff. This climb is rarely done. The symbol xx on the overview photo denotes anchor stations, not fixed gear anchors. Some anchors are gear.

Descent: Walk 100 meters south to tree. Rap to pins, then to ramp, move south to another station keeping a keen eye for the bolts on the outside of the ramp. Scramble down chimney. It may be easier just to walk off as per Cheese Stands Alone descent.

Access

Park at west Canyon Day Use Area and follow gravel road north for approximately 0.75 mile. Route is located on east facing wall just in front of prominent north-pointing buttress.

Note: Inquire at the ranger station concerning closures for nesting raptors prior to attempting this climb.

B. The Cheese Stands Alone 5.11b**

FA: M. Strassman
FFA: T. Goss, W. Harding

1st Pitch: Low angle ramp leads to two-pin anchor. (5.6, 50')

2nd Pitch: Varnish face climbing past five pins to two-pin anchor. (5.10, 65')

3rd Pitch: Runout mossy slab past two pins gains two-pin anchor. (5.8, 65')

Note: Retreat is probably impossible after this pitch

4th Pitch: Offwidth crack to left-leaning seam past four pins to two-pin anchor. (5.11b, 80')

5th Pitch: Hand cracks to varnish face and two-pin anchor. (5.9, 70')

6th Pitch: Varnish acmes past four pins to two-pin anchor at top of pedestal. (5.10a, 50')

7th Pitch: Friction slab past one pin in left facing corner to two pins at top.

Descent: Walk west to the top of the formation until it is possible to see the cliffs on the west side of Padre Canyon. Walk down steps on the ramps to the north and saddle drainage. (There are islands of trees and plants). Descend around dry falls, and take easiest looking slot canyon to the south. Follow drainage down boulders turning north again, then across a scary ledge and down chimney behind huge flake to canyon floor.

"Money will not purchase happiness for the man who has no concept of what he wants. Money will not give him a code of values, if he's evaded the knowledge of what to value, and it will not provide him with a purpose, if he's evaded the choice of what to seek. Money will not buy intelligence for the fool, or admiration for the coward, or respect for the incompetent." - Ayn Rand

Access

For the next several routes park at West Canyon Day Use Area and follow gravel road north for approximately 0.75 mile to where the Three Ponds Trail crosses the road. Follow the trail into the wash and exit to the left, gaining slickrock ledges to the base of the climbs.

Note: Inquire at the ranger station concerning closures for nesting raptors prior to attempting this climb.

C. Project
D. Fractured Rugosity 5.8* R

J. Tainio, M. Kindred

Thin and fragile varnish edging and crimps past three bolts to sling anchor. Sling acmes on initial runout section. (60')

E. Wagassa 5.8**

J. Tainio, M. Kindred, J. Visser

1st Pitch: From ledge with tree, left leaning crack past five bolts to sling anchor. (5.6, 80')

2nd Pitch: Traverse left then right on thin varnish acmes past three bolts to sling anchor. Sling acmes to reduce runouts. (5.8, 40')

3rd Pitch: Hand crack past block to top. (5.8, 60')

Descent: Downclimb chimney under block to north. Locate slung boulder. Two raps to ground. Slings on boulder are probably rotten by now.

Crawdad Canyon
Climbing Park

Todd Goss on Leap of Faith (5.13a)

CRAWDAD CANYON CLIMBING PARK

Imagine a canyon a mile long, with 60' high basalt cliffs so heavily featured that almost every inch is climbable at some level. A spring-fed mountain stream splashes between the roots of towering cottonwood trees, wind and birdsong compete for dominance. Walking from one crag to the next is a relaxing stroll through an enchanted wood.

Imagine what a climber could make of such a place. Picture brass plaques fixed to the base of each route, belay chairs, park benches, groomed belay platforms, and gym-like sport anchors making untying from the rope a thing of the past. Visualize hundreds of routes from warm-ups to desperates, slabs to roofs and everything in between. A fistfull of draws and a bus-load of motivation will go far in a place like this where route density exceeds climber density by 100 to 1 on almost any day of the week. Add a swimming pool with poolside service to bring tall cool drinks and well earned sustenance. Afterwards, game of billiards or beach volleyball would be a nice break for the fingertips. Lastly, you can retire in a lovely campsite near a waterfall fed cove in a forest glade.

That such a place exists seems too good to be true, yet this is no mere pipe dream. A paltry 20 miles north of St. George, Crawdad Canyon Rock Climbing Park is a climbers dream come true. This fantastic place is the result of the vision of Jim Bosse, who upon seeing 20 climbers in the hot sun at Black Rocks, set about finding some climbers to take a look at his canyon. He then provided the tools and encouragement to make his vision a reality.

In April 1996 Todd Goss and Curtis Strong put up the first route, and Goss spent most of the summer clearing vegetation and bolting new routes. Eventually Michal and Jen Nad, as well as the prolific Mike and Elizabeth Tupper, joined the fray and progress was made towards 100 routes. In 1998, Goss, Darl Biniaz and Erin Jones developed 40 routes in several areas downstream along with a trail system to access them.

Though Jim's passage in late '98 was a substantial loss to the climbing community, his wife Susan is committed to completing Jim's vision of creating the most unique rock climbing area in the world. Most visitors already find that vision a reality.

Season
Regular Season: May 1st to Labor Day, 9am-8pm. Seven days a week.
Winter Season: Labor Day to May 1st open by appointment only. Call (435) 574-2300 or (435) 574-2416 to make arrangements. The canyon runs east and west, so half of the canyon is in the shade at all times.

Access
Drive 20 miles north from St. George on Bluff St. which becomes Route 18. Just before crossing the bridge at the bottom of the hill, turn right at the rock sign for the park. Drive to the end of the road and park. Walk through the gate and down the hill to the office.

Camping
Drive in campsites (2) are available at $20.00 per night with a 20 person maximum limit per site. Walk-in sites are scattered throughout the canyon and are $10.00 per night per site.

CRAWDAD CANYON GUIDELINES

The owner of this park has invested much in the way of time and resources to make this area plush compared to other climbing destinations. Please follow these guidelines when using this area.

- Check in at the office, sign the liability waiver, and pay the entrance fee ($3.00 at present).
- All climbers under the age of 18 years of age must have the signature of a parent or guardian on the liability form.
- Bring a photo ID when signing in. You will be denied access to the park without it.
- No traditional climbing is allowed in the park.
- No bouldering or free soloing is allowed in the park.
- Do not tamper with any of the fixed equipment on the routes.
- Acts of vandalism will result in lifetime banishment from the park and criminal charges.
- A stick clip is recommended on routes where the first bolt hanger is painted yellow (one can be rented from the office).
- No children under the age of ten are allowed in climbing areas.
- No dogs allowed.
- Watch the profanity. Families come here too, and they don't want to watch you have a tantrum.

In Memoriam

Jim Bosse purchased Veyo pool resort in 1995. A true visionary in every sense of the word, Jim's plans for the canyon were near completion when he passed away in the fall of 1998.
He wanted to create something that didn't exist anywhere else — a beautiful parklike setting where a climber could wander from climb to climb along groomed trails in a magical forest, with the sounds of the birds in the trees competing with the splash and gurgle of the stream. Where dappled sunlight played on the cliff faces, and the wind rustled the trees at the top of the routes.

Jim worked hard to provide those experiences for us. He spent thousands of dollars to give us the opportunity to pursue our craft in a beautiful and comfortable place. He pulled weeds, trimmed trees, built trails, and burned brush piles. He provided chaise lounge chairs to belay from, brass plaques fixed to the base of each route, and sport anchors so we wouldn't have to untie at the top.

He grunted and sweated alongside those of us who shared his appreciation of the canyon, but would never come close to sharing his vision of what the canyon was to become. It is ironic that the most important person in the climbing community of southwestern Utah was a self-described non-climber.

Jim's contribution to the quality of the local climbing experience cannot be overstated, yet his contribution to the lives of those people who knew him was immeasurably greater.
Whether giving savvy business advice or dropping gems of wisdom like "never argue with stupid people," Jim seemed to be able to talk to anyone and raise the spirits of everyone around him.

Though Jim's spirit is everywhere in the canyon, his loss is sorely felt by those who knew him, and he will be missed by many.

CRAWDAD CANYON OVERVIEW

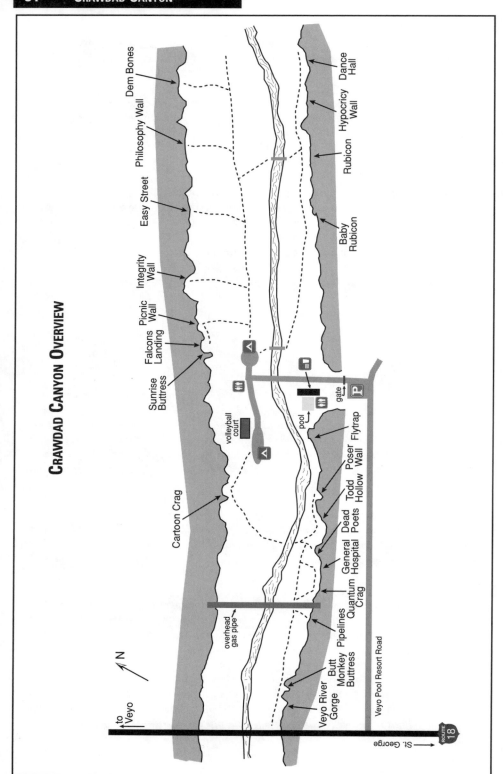

THE FLYTRAP

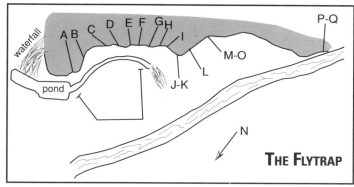

THE FLYTRAP

A. Superfly 5.9***

T. Goss

Climbs to top of ledge then up crack to short overhang. Big holds to sport anchors. Six bolts. (55')

B. Chef Sheri 5.8*

J. Bosse, T. Broderick

Jim's first and only climb. The first ascent done in jeans and tennis shoes. Five bolts lead up ledges and an arete. (40')

C. Fly Soup 5.7**

C. Strong, T. Goss

First route in the canyon. Edges and cracks to flake and jugs at top. Four bolts. (40')

D. Hopscotch 5.12b***

M. Nad, J. Nad

Six bolts up sweeping flake to roof. (50')

E. Metamorphosis 5.11a**

M. Nad, J. Nad

Reachy crimping and pockets through a bulge. Six bolts. (50')

F. The Fly 5.11c**

M. Nad, J. Nad

Steep and reachy crimping, easier ground above. Eight bolts. (65')

G. Ape Variation 5.12c**

M. Nad, J. Nad

A hard and crimpy start to route H. Nine bolts. (65')

H. Barking Crawdad 5.10c*

M. Nad, J. Nad

Awkward moves lead to nice climbing above. Seven bolts. (65')

I. Moucha 5.10b***

M. Nad, J. Nad

Czech for fly, one of the best on the crag. Stem to slab, to overhang to big holds. Eight bolts. (65')

J. The Deck Attraction 5.11b***

M. Nad, J. Nad

A strange start gives way to a swath cleaned through the moss up beautiful pockets. Seven bolts. (65')

K. Body language 5.11c*

M. Nad, J. Nad

Shares start with route J, Then up and right on the arete. Seven bolts. (65')

L. Lord of the Flies 5.12b**

M. Nad, J. Nad

Pull the prominent roof on crimps, then up pockets to a rap anchor. Eight bolts. (65')

M. Czenglish Master 5.10d**

M. Nad, J. Nad

A mix of Czech and English. Nice stemming past eight bolts to rap anchor. (65')

N. Hate Crimes 5.12b

T. Goss, A. Jones

Jim said, "Well can't you use that drill and make some holds?" Work up the corner then up arete with a pair of glued-on holds. Six bolts to rap anchor. (65')

O. Lagoon 5.10b*

M. Nad, J. Nad

When you pull the cord you'll understand the name. Corner to nice face. Seven bolts. (65')

P. Learning to Fly 5.12c***

T. Goss, E. Jones

Flared corner to reachy moves over a roof. Seven bolts to rap anchors. (65')

Q. The Prow 5.11c**

M. Nad, D. Biniaz

Shares start with P, then moves up the blunt arete. Seven bolts. (65')

THE CARTOON CRAG

A. Greased Scotsman 5.9*

T. Goss, C. Strong
Climb through blocks to the pocketed face passing three bolts. (35')
Note: The one bolt variation to the left is 5.10a.

B. Animated Frustration 5.10b**

T. Goss, N. Shields
Nice pockets and ledges to a balancy finish. Three bolts. (35')

C. Beating Up a Cripple 5.11c**

T. Goss, T. Broderick
Four bolts through an overhang with big holds. (35')

D. Tasmanian Twist 5.8*

T. Goss, T. Broderick
Edges and big holds follow four bolts to sport anchors. (35')

E. Strung Out Charlie Brown 5.11c**

T. Goss, J. Truelove
Crimps and pockets punctuate an ever-steepening face. Five bolts to chains. (40')

F. Wacked out Lucy 5.11d*

T. Goss, W. Harding

Nice face climbing leads to sloper crux. Five bolts to chains. (40')

G. Ego Massage 5.8*

M. Nad, J. Nad

Nice stemming corner past five bolts. (40')

H. Barney With an Attitude 5.9**

T. Goss, J. Truelove

Blocky face to nice face climbing. Four bolts. (40')

I. Homerpalooza 5.12a**

T. Goss, W. Harding

A one move wonder. Thin holds on roof to huge jug. Climb around crux and route is 5.11a. Four bolts. (40')

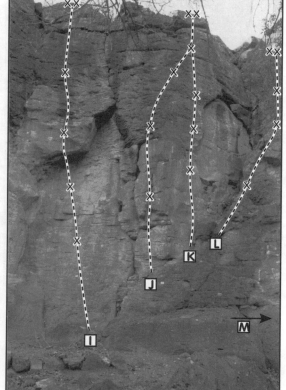

J. Butthead 5.10c*

T. Goss, J. Towt

Cracked pillar to pocketed face. Four bolts. (35')

K. Beavis 5.10a*

T. Goss, J. Towt

Edges and pockets past four bolts to shared rap anchor. (35')

L. Smurfs On Steroids 5.10a

T. Goss, J. Truelove

Follow the ramp to an awkward and short face. Three bolts, to rap anchor. (30')

M. Bar-B-Que 5.10a**

M. Nad, J. Nad

Blocky edges past five bolts. (40')

TODD HOLLOW

A. Farmers Daughter 5.9*

> *T. Goss, T. Broderick*
> Through loose mossy start to nice edges above. Four bolts. (35')

B. Mother Goose 5.9*

> *T. Goss, E. Jones*
> Blocky to steep pockets in convex face. Four bolts to anchors. (35')

C. Brothers Keeper 5.10b**

> *T. Goss, T. Broderick*
> Blocky start to short bulge. Four bolts. (35')

D. Cousin It 5.11b**

> *T. Goss, T. Broderick*
> Nice arete climb on good pockets and edges. Four bolts. (35')

E. Father Time 5.10c***

> *T. Goss, R. Goss*
> Face to right of arete. Pockets and edges past four bolts. (35')

F. Native Son 5.10d***

> *T. Goss, R. Goss*
> Steep arete, aesthetic moves, good rock. Four bolts. (35')

G. Sibling Rivalry 5.10b**

> *T. Goss, E. Jones*
> Face climbing past four bolts with reachy crux. Rap anchors. (35')

H. Family Planning 5.9**

> *T. Goss, E. Jones*
> Stemming in a dihedral with a crack. Four bolts to G's anchors. (35')

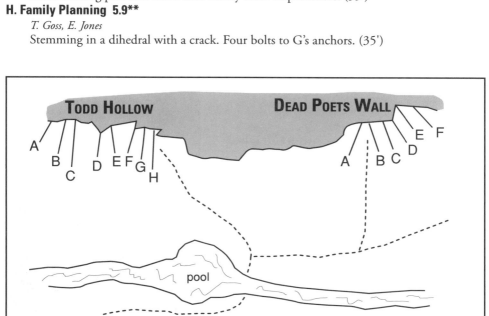

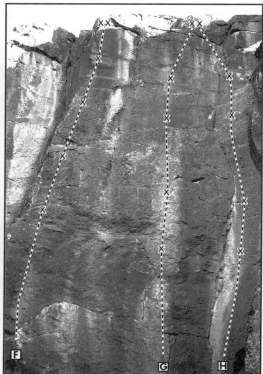

THE POSER WALL

A. Project

B. Little Princess 5.6 *

J. Posman, T. Broderick
Blocky edges and pockets past three bolts to sport anchor. (30')

C. H.M.G. (High Maintenance Girl) 5.5
Mossy slab to horizontal cracks. Two bolts. (25')

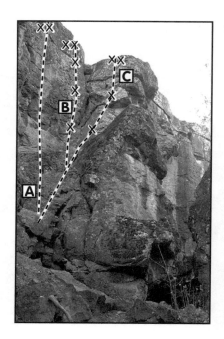

THE DEAD POETS CRAG

A. Project

B. Talking of Michelangelo 5.11c**

D. Biniaz, T. Goss

C. Ignoble Strife 5.12b**

T. Goss, D. Biniaz

Steep pockets to small crimping.
Stick clip needed. Four bolts. (40')

D. Nevermore 5.11d**

T. Goss, E. Jones

Through overhang on good pockets
to crack. Stick clip needed. Five
bolts. (40')

E. Constantly Risking Absurdity 5.10c**

D. Biniaz, T. Goss

Deceptively tricky stemming corner.
Four bolts to sport anchor. (40')

**F. Slouching Towards Bethlehem
5.10c****

T. Goss, D. Binaz

Sharp pockets through reachy bulge.
Four bolts to rap anchor. (45')

THE GENERAL HOSPITAL

A. Project

B. Hemorrhagic Fever 5.10c***

T. Goss, D. Biniaz

Sharp arete with nice pockets. Four bolts. (40')

C. Ebola 5.10b**

T. Goss, D. Biniaz

Pockets in a steep face with committing finish. Three bolts. (40')

D. Anti-Bodies 5.9+*

T. Goss, D. Biniaz

Mossy slab to nice face with big ledge. Three bolts to rap anchor. (35')

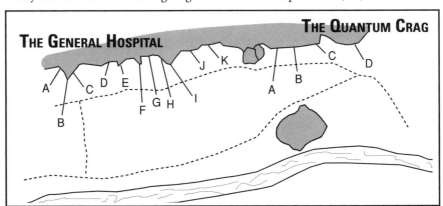

Michael Nad on Hemorrhagic Fever (5.10c)

E. Viral Pandemic 5.10c*

T. Goss, D. Biniaz

Slab start to nice arete with awkward moves. Four bolts. (35')

F. Occam's Razor 5.11b**

T. Goss, E. Jones

Blocky climbing to sharp arete. Four bolts. (40')

G. Infarctions don't Stink 5.9+**

T. Goss, D. Biniaz

Nice warm up with a mossy start to nice pockets. Four bolts to sport anchor (40')

H. Mitosis Hurts 5.10b**

E. Jones, T. Goss

Cleaned slab, to letter box pockets – nice route. Four bolts. (40')

I. Double Amputee 5.10a**

T. Goss, D. Binaz

Blunt arete with edges and pockets on both sides. Four bolts to rap anchor. (45')

J. Precardial Thump 5.10d***

T. Goss, E. Jones

Nice face climbing past four bolts to big hueco at rap anchor. (40')

K. Project

THE QUANTUM CRAG

A. Uncertainty Principle 5.11a***

> *T. Goss, D. Biniaz*
> Edges to big roof with glued on holds. Four bolts. (40')

B. Project

C. Project

D. Scholdlinglers Cat 5.12a**

> *T. Goss, E. Jones*
> Some of the coolest pockets in the canyon. Five bolts. (45')

THE PIPELINES

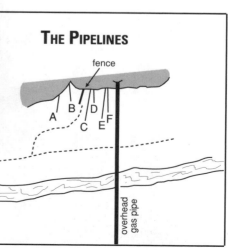

THE PIPELINES

A. Put That in Your Pipe and Smoke it 5.9+**

T. Goss, D. Biniaz
Broken pillar to nice pockets and hard finish. Four bolts to sport anchor. (40')

B. Crack Pipe 5.8**

D. Biniaz, T. Goss
Nice corner past four bolts to shared rap anchor. 40'

C. Pipe Dreams 5.10a***

D. Biniaz, T. Goss
Pockets and edges up steep face past five bolts to sport anchor. (40')

D. Laying Pipe 5.8**

T. Goss, D. Biniaz
Rising left traverse up pockets past five bolts to sport anchor. (40')

E. Pipe Stem 5.9*

T. Goss, D. Biniaz
Good stemming corner past five bolts to sport anchor. Shares first two bolts with route D. (40')

F. Pipe Down 5.9*

T. Goss, D. Biniaz
Low angled arete to slab finish. Four bolts shares anchor with E. (40')

THE BUTT MONKEY BUTTRESS

A. Little Rat Bastards 5.12a**

T. Goss E. Jones
Pockets and edges in a face to an overhanging corner. Thin crack then across face. Five bolts. (50')

B. Project

C. Flying Butt Monkeys 5.12c**

T. Goss, D. Biniaz
Thin face to hand traverse then up steep arete. Seven bolts. (50')

D. Baboon Mentality 5.12b**

T. Goss, E. Jones
Slab to face and arete on great pockets. Six bolts. (55')

THE VEYO RIVER GORGE (AKA THE VRG)

A. Bend Over Dorothy 5.11a**
D. Biniaz, T. Goss
Edges to small roof on good holds. Four bolts. (40')

B. Monkeyshines 5.12a*
D. Biniaz, T. Goss
Steep face to reachy corner. Four bolts. (40')

C. Project

D. Stop Saying "Dude" 5.10d**
D. Biniaz, T. Goss
Dusty edges to nice pockets and difficult finish. Four bolts. (40')

E. I Saw Jesus at K-Mart 5.12b**
T. Goss, E. Jones
Short steep face of nice edges. Four bolts. (40')

F. Warm and Fuzzy 5.6
D. Biniaz, T. Goss
Moss climbing....bring crampons. Four bolts and sport anchors. (40')

SUNRISE BUTTRESS

Note: No photos for A-E

A. Horseshoe 5.11b**
M. Nad, T. Broderick
Scramble up blocks to pockets on arete. Four bolts. (40')

B. Gaper Crack 5.10b**
M. Nad, T. Broderick
Nice crack near corner. Four bolts to a shared rap anchor. (40')

C. Fun in the Sun 5.10d**
M. Nad, T. Broderick
Fun moves with reachy crux (harder if your short). Five bolts. (50')

D. Sunrise Buttress 5.10a***
T. Broderick, M. Nad
Shares first bolt with C then up gorgeous arete with bucket holds. Seven bolts. (50')

E. Road to the Sun 5.8***
T. Broderick, M. Nad
Nice climbing on discontinuous cracks in clean steep face. Five bolts to sport anchors. (50')

FALCONS LANDING

A. Dallas 5.12a**
I. Horn
Steep scoop on pockets to easier ground above. Four bolts. (45')

B. Knotts Landing 5.10c**
I Horn, T. Nguyen
Five bolts lead through great edges and pockets on this clean face. Rap anchor. (45')

C. Dynasty 5.8**
T. Nguyen, A. Deckert
Stem using leaning block then big holds past five bolts to sport anchor. (45')

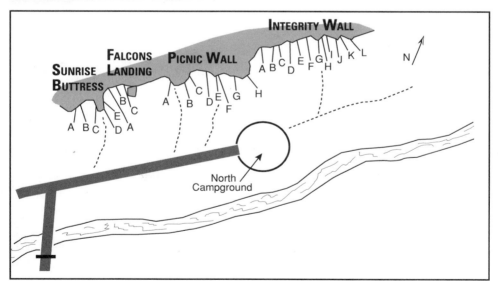

THE PICNIC WALL

A. Catwalk 5.7***
T. Broderick, M. Nad
Excellent beginner lead on big edges. Six bolts and sport anchor. (55')

B. Gape Index 5.10c*
M. Nad, J. Nad
Boulder problem followed by nice moves up pillar. Five bolts. (55')

Brandon Beck on Catwalk (5.7)

C. Jumping Jimney 5.10c**
FA Unknown
Starts up corner then nice face
moves to reachy finish. Six bolts to
shared rap anchor with B. (55')

D. Bag Lunch 5.8**
T. Goss, M. Nad
Big horizontal holds to steeper
section with pockets. Five bolts to
sport anchor. (55')

E. Mojo Roof 5.11a*
T. Goss, R. Fisher
Arete moves to short roof with big
holds. Six bolts. (55')

F. Hot Tin Roof 5.11a*
T. Goss, T. Broderick
Shares 1st three bolts of E, then
straight up through edges to big
roof holds. Six bolts. (55')

G. Ransom Demand 5.10a*
T. Goss, B. Ransom
Thin edgy start to awkward reachy
moves. Five bolts. (55')

H. Paradigm Shift 5.12b**
T. Goss, M. Nad
Nice sculpted rock through roof
and six bolts. (55')

THE INTEGRITY WALL

A. Firestorm 5.10a

T. Goss, E. Jones

Located to the left of A. Not pictured. Pockets and edges to flake (scary) and big holds. Five bolts to rap anchors. (40')

B. Hotdog Philosophy 5.10a*

M. Nad, T. Broderick

Bouldery start to nice edges. Four bolts to chains. (35')

C. Picnic Dudes 5.11b*

M. Nad, T. Broderick

Thin edgy start, with sloping pockets to finish. Continue past the chains at the top of route B. Six bolts. (50')

D. Talk the Talk 5.10c**

T. Goss, T. Broderick

Stem up corner left of the arete past four bolts. (If you climb exclusively on the arete route is 11a). (45')

E. Walk the Walk 5.10a**

T. Goss, J. Truelove

If you can't walk the walk, don't talk the talk. Five bolts. (45')

F. No Holds Barred 5.11d**

T. Goss, J. Truelove

Thin feet to layback, and pockets. Five bolts. (50')

G. High Fidelity 5.11d***

T. Goss, J. Truelove

Beautiful pocketed arete with hard to clip anchor. Four bolts. (45')

H. Honor Amongst Trees 5.11a**

T. Goss, T. Broderick

Thin edging to killer pockets and hard finish. Four bolts. (45')

I. Integrity 5.11c**

M. Nad, J. Nad

Stem the corner to reachy pockets. Five bolts. (50')

J. Truth and Consequence 5.11a**

T. Goss, I. Horn

Thin friction slab to nice arete. Four bolts. (50')

K. Stemming the Tide 5.10a**

R. Fisher, T. Goss

Excellent stemming corner past five bolts. (50')

L. Round Two 5.10d*

> *I. Horn, T. Goss*
> Difficult start to nice face climbing. Three bolts. (35')

EASY STREET

A. Project

B. Project

C. Mr. Bubbly 5.11b*

> *L. Ierian, M. Ierian*
> Blocky start leads to small roof
> and rap anchor. Four bolts. (30')

D. Hail on the Chief 5.12b/c**

> *M. Tupper, T. Broderick*
> First ascent done in the middle
> of a hailstorm. Four bolts. (30')

E. Chilled Bubbly 5.11c**

> *M. Ierian, M. Tupper*
> Shares first bolt with D then three more. (30')

THE PHILOSOPHY WALL

A. Nested Holons 5.10a**

> *T. Goss, E. Jones*
> Vertical face climbing to easier
> pockets. Four bolts. (40')

B. Utopia 5.6**

> *T. Goss, E. Jones*
> Crack left of the arete, to buckets.
> Clip the four bolts on route C.
> Sport anchor. (40')

C. Transcend and Include 5.9***

> *T. Goss, E. Jones*
> Great introduction to aretes. Four
> bolts to sport anchor. (40')

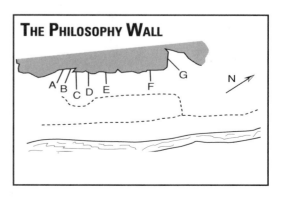

D. Mystics of Spirit 5.10a**

T. Goss, E. Jones
Excellent pocket climbing on blunt arete. Four bolts to sport anchor. (40')

E. Mystics of Muscle 5.10b

T. Goss, E. Jones
Loose start to sinker pockets in water streak. Four bolts. (40')

F. Who Says You Kant 5.6***

T. Goss, E. Jones
Great rock on this slab with a crack. Four bolts. (40')

G. Primacy of Existence 5.10c***

T. Goss, E. Jones
Edges, roof, pockets, crack. What more is there? Five bolts. (45')

DEM BONES WALL

A. Operation 5.12c***

M. Tupper, M. Ierian
Crack, layback, and undercling, past five bolts. (35')

B. Surgery 5.13b**

M. Tupper
Thin, reachy, crimpy moves past five bolts. (40')

C. The Procedure 5.11d***

M. Ierian, M. Tupper
Nice variety of holds past five bolts. (40')

D. Dumb Bonehead 5.10b**

M. Nad, D. Biniaz
Edges and pockets up beautiful rock. Five bolts. (40')

E. Project

THE DANCE HALL

A. Eighties No More 5.11c**

M. Nad, R. Fisher
Couldn't stand the 80's music at the pool anymore. Five bolts. (45')

B. Dirty Dancing 5.8*

R. Fisher, M. Nad
Stemming in the corner past five bolts. (45')

C. Homeboy Macarena 5.11d**

M. Nad, R. Fisher
Nice rock on this edgy and pocket route. Five bolts. (45')

D. Last Dance 5.11c**

M. Nad, R. Fisher
Pockets in a bulge to edges above. Five bolts. (45')

E. Electric Watusi 5.12a/b**

T. Goss, M. Tupper
Small overhang to sinker pockets and flake. Five bolts. (45')

F. Sanduco 5.12b**

T. Goss, I. Horn
Slab to steep pockets with crimpy finish. Five bolts. (45')

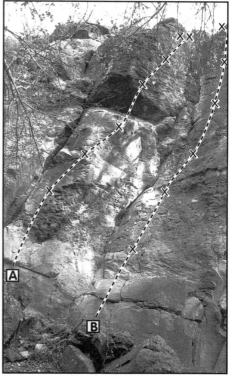

THE HYPOCRISY WALL

A. Polka 5.12b★★

    M. Nad, J. Nad

    Smooth wall of edges to great pockets in bulge. Four bolts to rap anchor. (45')

B. Cactus Blues 5.12c★★

    M. Nad, T. Goss

    Pockets and incut edges to reachy crimps. Four bolts. (45')

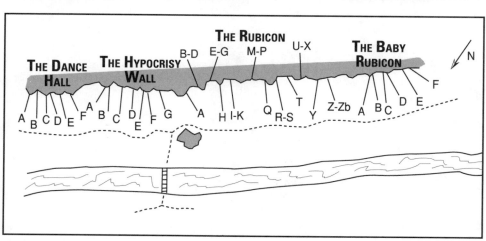

C. Infidelity 5.11d**

T. Goss, M. Tupper

Sloper start to good pockets. Nice rock. Five bolts. (45')

D. Project

E. Mrs. Hypocrite 5.12b*

M. Nad, J. Nad

Steep pocketed start to easier edges. Five bolts. No picture. (45')

F. Mr. Hypocrite 5.11b**

M. Nad, T. Broderick

Flake to cracks above. Six bolts. No picture. (45')

G. The Asylum 5.12a*

M. Nad, T. Broderick

Awkward and crimpy. Six bolts. No picture. (50')

THE RUBICON

A. The Forgotten Corner 5.10c**

M. Nad, J. Nad

Crimpy slab to nice corner. Six bolts to anchor on route B. (55')

B. Aerial Dentistry 5.13a***

M. Tupper, T. Goss

Steep crimping on this sustained and reachy route. Five bolts to rap anchor. (50')

C. Victim of Circumstance 5.11b**

T. Goss, J. Truelove

Edges and sidepulls to crack. Six bolts to rap anchor. (50')

D. Burning Bridges 5.12a***

T. Goss, J. Truelove

Sustained pocket pulling to sloper finish. Seven bolts to rap anchor. (55')

E. Owed to An Open Mind 5.13b/c

T. Perkins

Small edges and tiny pockets past six bolts to anchor. (55')

F. I Climb Therefore I Sweat 5.11d**

M. Nad, T. Goss

Stemming in corner with pockets. Six bolts to rap anchor. (50')

G. I Stink Therefore I Am 5.11b***

J. Nad, M. Nad

Flake to pockets in bulge. Six bolts to rap anchor. (50')

H. Narcolepsy 5.8*

E. Tuper, M. Tupper

Up pillar on reachy but big holds. Four bolts to sport anchor. (40')

I. Project

J. Leap of Faith 5.13a***

T. Goss, M. Tupper

Pockets to blind dyno then edges to top. Seven bolts to rap anchor. (55')

K. Rubicon 5.12b**

M. Tupper, E. Tupper

Crack climbing to big overhanging block. Seven bolts to rap anchor. (55')

L. Irreconcilable Differences 5.13b**

M. Nad, J. Nad

Good pockets to small but reachy slopers. Six bolts to rap anchor. (55')

M. Kissing Chi Chi's Ass 5.12a**

M. Nad. J. Nad

A reference to a demanding cat. Shares five bolts with N. Seven bolts to rap anchor. (55')

N. Pushing Sport Climbing 5.11a**

J. Nad, M. Nad

Handcrack to traverse on arete. Seven bolts to rap anchor. (55')

O. Gypsy Dance 5.12d***

M. Nad, J. Nad

Pockets to flake to shared rap anchor with route N. Seven bolts. (55')

Note: A variation climbs above the flake on smaller holds – same grade.

P. The Reckoning 5.12b**

T. Goss, M. Nad

Begins on route O. Finger crack to edges on face and up a small roof. Seven bolts to rap anchor. (55')

Q. Rude Awakening 5.12c***

T. Goss, M. Nad

Bulge to arete to roof. Seven bolts to rap anchor. (55')

R. Just Say No To Posing 5.12c***

M. Nad, J. Nad

Pocketed arete past seven bolts to rap anchor. (55')

S. Return of the Jedi 5.11b**

T. Goss, M. Tupper

Stemming corner with sharp edges past five bolts to rap anchor. (55')

T. Where Is Your Messiah Now? 5.11d

M. Nad, J. Nad

Steep scoop to edgy face above. Six bolts to rap anchor. (50')

U. Toxic Emotions 5.11b*

T. Goss, J. Truelove
Reachy pockets that wander across face. Six bolts to rap anchor. (50')

V. Sparkle and Fade 5.11a**

I. Horn, S. Sarver
Hand crack to nice edges. Good warm-up. Five bolts to rap anchor. (50')

W. Manifest Destiny 5.12a***

T. Goss, J. Truelove
Awesome rock on sculpted edges, pockets and jugs. Seven bolts to rap anchor. (55')

X. The Talisman 5.12d***

T. Goss, J. Truelove
Shares 1st two bolts with W, then up a burly double undercling to nice pockets. Reconnects with W at top. Six bolts total to rap anchor. (55')

Y. Hard Cranking Dude 5.11c*

M. Nad, J. Nad
Stemming and edges past five bolts to rap anchor. (55')
Note: If you climb it as a crack climb it's 5.9 or so.

Z. Monkey Business 5.11b/c***

J. Nad, M. Nad
Starts on Y for 1st bolt, then moves to a crack. An overhanging hand traverse leads to pockets to top. Five bolts to rap anchor. (55')

Za. Veyo Quickie 5.12b**

M. Nad, J. Nad
Steep and technical on this short route. Four bolts to rap anchor. (50')

Zb. Slash and Burn 5.11a

T. Goss, J. Truelove

Wanders around a lot, not a great route. Six bolts to rap anchor. (55')

BABY RUBICON

A. Calypso 5.10a**

E. Tupper, M. Tupper

Stem and layback corner to small crimpy pockets. Four bolts to rap anchor. (50')

B. Project

C. Morning Sickness 5.11c*

I. Horn, J. Towt

Blocky start to nice pockets. Four bolts to rap anchor. Not pictured. (50')

D. Project

E. Spit Shine 5.7**

J. Truelove, T. Goss

Ramp to slab with incut edges and pockets. Four bolts to sport anchor. (35')

F. Subject to Change 5.7**

J. Truelove, J. Truelove

Ramp to slab then big holds on steep finish. Four bolts to sport anchor. (35')

UTAH HILLS

Darl Biniaz on Petrified (5.10c)

UTAH HILLS

A number like 325 million years seems easy to grasp when you are standing in line at the Department of Motor Vehicles. Yet under ordinary circumstances geologic time scales are hard to imagine. Back that long ago the limestone we climbers so merrily clamber on was nothing more than scum on the bottom of a shallow sea. Eons of detritus were crushed and compressed; uplifted by block faulting; and eroded by water, wind, and time. The stone has matured like a fine wine, ready to be uncorked and enjoyed — a light, yet unpretentious little limestone, with a fine Mississippian aftertaste.

No longer at sea level, the Utah Hills crags lie at the boundary of the Mojave and Great Basin deserts, where the silence of sage and juniper is interrupted only by the wind and ravens. (The occasional low moan of a free range cow adds a special Western effect).

Accessed by dozens of mining roads, the approaches are either casual or terrifying depending on the condition of their surfaces. The numerous crags of the Utah Hills offer over a hundred routes scattered over eight areas. From savage mini-routes like The Present to the multi-pitch outings on the Diamond, climbers will enjoy variety, quality, and solitude.

Climbers from all over the state of Utah have added to the development of this area. As a testament to the quality of stone, climbers drive five hours to drill a dozen bolts. The pioneering effort of these climbers is, at least, impressive, and at best, worthy of sainthood. We can show our appreciation by enjoying the fruits of their labors and by leaving the area cleaner than we found it.

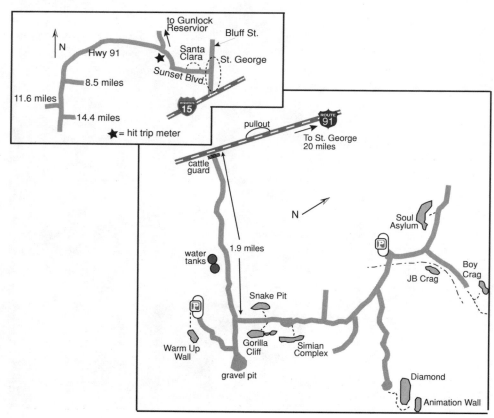

GORILLA CLIFFS

With the discovery of the awesome potential of the Virgin River Gorge in 1989, climbers from both Salt Lake City and Las Vegas began to look for similar formations in the Beaver Dam Mountains to the west of St. George. They didn't have to look very hard to discover the incredible wealth of exposed limestone in almost every direction. Climbers from both Las Vegas and Salt Lake City began to develop the routes on Gorilla Cliff in early 1990. Armed with a low power Bosch drill, Mike Tupper recalls drilling routes less than three bolts at a time before retreating to Las Vegas to recharge batteries during the cold winter months. Many of the longer routes on the right side of the formation were bolted throughout the early 90's as well as several projects which remain futuristic and uncompleted even today. As other climbers from Salt Lake heard about the endless limestone walls of the area, the gaps in the wall began to be filled in and attention turned to the short but steep formations to the left of the main wall. Too high to boulder, these thuggish, sometimes sharp and burly mini-routes are typically two to four bolts in length and culminate in The Present, which at 5.14a is the hardest route in the area.

Season

Gorilla Cliff faces true north and never receives any appreciable sunlight. With an elevation of 5000' this wall is climbable all year round though some winter days may be too cold and summer afternoons may offer conditions too hot for micro-crimping.

Access

Take Sunset Blvd. west off Bluff Street in St. George and head 10.7 miles west through the town of Santa Clara, past the turn for Ivins, and out into the Shivwits Reservation. Bear left at the Gunlock turnoff (hit your trip meter) and travel west for 8.5 miles (you will have crested Utah Hill and passed the microwave tower on the left). Turn left onto a gravel road crossing a yellow cattle guard, and continue another 1.9 miles to an intersection. Turn left and continue 0.2 mile and park at a small pullout on the right about 100 yards past the wall. Walk back down the road and locate the trail marked with a cairn.

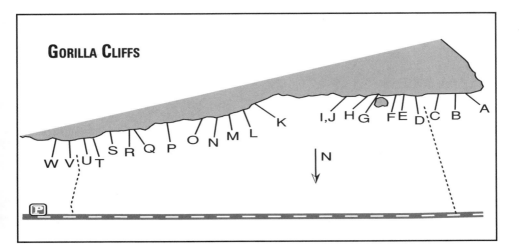

GORILLA CLIFFS

A. Gorilla 5.13b*

G. Weigand

Jump to hueco then move right onto thin pocketed face and thin slab to anchor. Six bolts. (60')

B. This Side of Paradise 5.11d**

C. Reason

Through huecos which make a gorilla face, around roof and bush to slab. Six bolts to chains. Bravery can help you with the runout. (65')

C. Nintendo 5.13c**

G. Weigand

From stacked blocks climb up gray streak on crimps and powerful sidepulls. Five bolts to a common anchor with route B. (65')

D. Project

E. Project

F. Project

G. Country Boy 5.12d**

M. Tupper

From the top of the block, head up pinches and crimps then along the prow right of white streak. Five bolts to chains. (60') *Tupper said he always had intentions of moving the boulder with a car jack but other routes beckoned.*

H. Just Left of Paradise 5.11b***

M. Tupper, C. Reason

Bigger holds on superb rock wigh a technical slab at the top. Seven bolts to chains. (65')

I. Winter Dance 5.12c**

M. Tupper

Shares first two bolts of route J up small pockets in bulge to shared anchor with H. Six bolts to chains. (65')

J. Glass Slipper 5.12a**

M. Tupper

Grey and gold streaks provide pinches, pockets, and edges past six bolts to chains. (65')

K. Mike Calls' Route 5.12c/d*
M. Call
Small pockets and sidepulls on smooth gray rock past three bolts to anchor. (35')

L. The Realm 5.13b/c**
T. Kemple
Thin and awkward moves through three bolts to chains. (40')

M. The Present 5.14a***
B. Speed
Crimps and small pockets trending left on this short but powerful classic. Three bolts to chains on ledge. You may also clip a directional. (30')

N. Warm Up Route 5.12c/d*
FA unknown
Follow two bolts up small pockets through overhang to ledge with chains. (25')

O. 5.11c*
E. Decaria
Edges and sidepulls up shallow dihedral. Three bolts to rap anchor. (30')

P. Lucky #13 5.11a*
B. Meecham
Pockets in a gray slab moving right to rap anchor. Four bolts. (35')

Q. Fosters in the Morning 5.11d*
B. Meecham
Blocky sidepulls and pinches past three bolts to shared anchor. (25')

R. Spanking Monkey 5.12b**
E. Decaria
Crimping up nice streaked rock. Shares start and anchor with route Q. Three bolts to anchor. (25')

S. Ankle Breaker 5.12c*
FA unknown
Up grey streak past crimps and pockets. Three bolts to anchor. The name may be appropriate if you blow the 3rd clip! (30')

T. Missing Link 5.11?
FA unknown
Six feet left of route S. Edges through a scoop to anchor. Three bolts. (30')

U. Project

V. 5.11a*

> *E. Decaria*
>
> Low angle edging to stem dihedral and pocketed face to chains. Four bolts. (35')

W. Silverback 5.10

> *FA unknown*
>
> Twenty feet left of V. Two bolts in a pocketed slab to chains. (25')

THE SNAKEPIT

Just across the road from the Gorilla Cliff are a series of fire blackened caves underneath a nicely featured wall. Optimistically bolted several years ago, the moves through the nearly featureless roofs proved rather futuristic, and the routes remained as projects. Lured to the sun-baked wall by the cold and windy conditions at the other crags in the area, Salt Lake City locals Tim Roberts, Jeff Baldwin, and Lee Logston began climbing the routes by winching through the first few moves to enjoy the climbing above. Realizing the potential of this nice wall, several other climbs were redpointed using the winch start and designated A0. The crag now offers several routes in the 5.11 to 5.12 grades with all day sunshine as a bonus.

Season

September through May are the best times for The Snakepit, with cold winter afternoons being optimal. There may be a 20 degree temperature difference between this wall and the Gorilla Cliff across the street. In the summer this wall bakes; don't bother.

Access

Follow the directions for Gorilla Cliffs, and park in the same location. The crag is across the road.

Note: It's possible the accuracy of this wall's name derives from the presence of a rattlesnake den in the caves. Rattlesnakes are a likely site, and visitors in the spring should use appropriate caution, especially considering that this is the habitat of the Mojave Green rattlesnake subspecies.

THE SNAKEPIT

A. Science Diet 5.12a**
T. Roberts

Flake to pockets in corner of roof moving right to seam with pockets then through roof to higher chains. Nine bolts. (60')

B. Bitten 5.12a*
T. Roberts

Direct start to A that moves under roof and departs left to separate anchor. Nine bolts to chains. (55')

C. Sidewinder 5.13a**
T. Roberts

Cairn start leads to blocky sidepulls and steep crimpy face through small roof. Hard boulder problem down low. Nine bolts to chains. (65')

D. Snake Juice 5.12c A0**
J. Baldwin

Winch start leads to huecos and departs left through steep face and joins route C. Ten bolts to chains. (60')

E. Sunking 5.13a**
E. Decaria

Winch start attains awesome huecos and jugs to chains. Seven bolts and shares anchor with D. Start freed by Will Smith. (45')

F. Winch Boy 5.11a A0*
T. Roberts

Winch start to crimps and pockets in very nice rock. Eight bolts to chains. (60')

G. Dead Man Chalking 5.12d**
T. Roberts

Steep roof moves to crimps in dihedral, then bulge and slab to chain anchor. Seven bolts. (50')

H. Nemesis 5.12b**
L. Logston

Pockets in dihedral lead to face moves and chains. Seven bolts. (50')

I. Prickler 5.11a
T. Roberts

Black streak with very sharp crimps and pockets. Four bolts to chains. (40')

J. Sega 5.11a*
T. Roberts

Blocky sidepulls to ledge and easy moves to chains. Five bolts. (40')

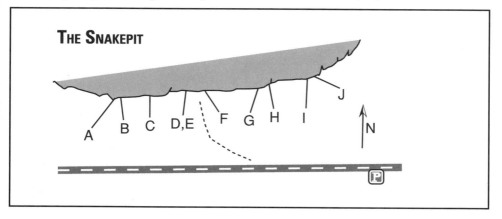

THE SIMIAN COMPLEX

Rising above the low trees in front of the parking area, the Simian Complex is predominately blocky limestone with the occasional pocket thrown in for variety.

Developed by an eclectic mix of climbers from Moab, Salt Lake City and St. George, this wall has been both praised as excellent and dissed as sharp and dirty. This is probably due to the blocky features on the wall which require much pinching and body tension on somewhat sharp rock. The proximity to the smooth pockets of the Gorilla Cliff and Snake Pit, both of which seem to be more user friendly by comparison, may also be a factor. Comparisons aside, this is an aesthetic and secluded crag with nicely developed routes on beautifully streaked limestone.

Season
With a northerly aspect, The Simian Complex is climbable most of the year, though summer afternoons may be a bit too warm due to the low elevation. The best seasons are fall, winter and early spring.

Access
Follow the directions for the Gorilla Cliff. Park and continue up the road for 50 meters to the access trail; the wall is only thirty seconds away from here.

Note: There is a beautiful red pictograph in a recess at the center of the cliff. The routes have been engineered to go nowhere near this rock art. Please do not boulder or climb anywhere near this area! Also, do not touch or in any way deface this rare and delicate voice of the past.

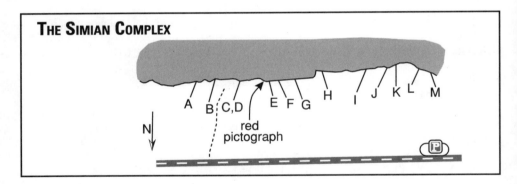

THE SIMIAN COMPLEX

A. The Gray Streak 5.12b/c**
FA unknown
Blocky edges up beautiful streak past four bolts to chains. (45')

B. Stolen Sunset 5.12b/c**
M. Tupper, E. Tupper
Blocky dihedral tending left onto prow and steep face to open coldshuts. Six bolts. (50')

C. Ball and Chain 5.12b**
K. Oldrid, M. Call
Blocky overhang 20' left of the pictograph. Sharp blocks through gray and tan streaks. Five bolts to chains. (50')

D. Barrel of Monkeys 5.12d
FA unknown

A variation to the right of the third bolt of C then back to the same anchors. Seven bolts. (50')

E. Ape Index 5.12d*
Mike Tupper

Fifteen feet to right of pictograph, crimpy blocks moving right to left. Five bolts to open coldshuts. (50')

F. Bedtime for Bonzo 5.12c
FA unknown

Blocky pinches and pockets up blunt prow to chains on ledge. Five bolts. (45')

G. 5.12a
E. Decaria

Steep and blocky moves at the start lead to easier ground above. Four bolts to chains. (45')

H. Santa Clara Warm-Up 5.10b*
FA unknown

Sidepulls and pinches on large holds to sharp pockets at top. Four bolts to chains. (45')

I. 5.11d*
B. Hadley

Left of large hueco, up prominent gray streak on crimps and pockets through overhang to chains. Five bolts. (40')

J. Stolen Dream 5.12b/c**
L. Logston

Right of hueco, pinches and edges right to blocky overhang. Four bolts to rap anchor. (40')

K. Nic-O-Fit 5.12d/13a**
B. Mecham

Short route moving left to right on blocky crimps and pinches. Three bolts to chains. (30')

L. Monkeyshines 5.12b***
FA unknown

Ten feet to left of hueco, small pockets and pinches lead past three bolts to chains. (35')

M. Natural Selection 5.11a/b***
FA unknown

Short weaving route up gray and tan streaks. Five bolts to chains. (40')

Jennifer Nad on White Soul Power (5.12a)

THE SOUL ASYLUM

Sometimes the best crags are in the most unexpected locations. With so much stone readily visible in the vast Utah Hills area, it is surprising that a hidden crag like the Soul Asylum didn't take ten years to discover.

Searching for sustained and fingery routes similar to the short routes on The Gorilla Cliff, Kelly Oldrid and Mike Call found the Soul Asylum lurking around an unlikely looking hillside just off a 4WD road. The pair quickly put up the Ren and Stimpy Wall on the left side of the formation, and word got out about the great potential of the remainder of the area.

Lee Logston and Jeff Baldwin developed the fantastic pocketed routes on the right side of the formation (the belays for which are in wonderful hanging and shaded alcoves). Logston began work on the steep routes in the center of the wall next with contributions by Jeff Baldwin, Lange Jefferies, Tim Roberts, Nancy McCullough, Todd Goss, and Darl Biniaz.

The climbing at The Soul Asylum varies from the overhanging smooth pockets of White Soul Power, to the pure friction slab climbing of Happy Happy. It is the first developed limestone area in the region to provide well protected, aesthetic routes with moderate grades, and is a good destination for groups with climbers of varied experience.

Season
The wall has an east-southeast aspect, and receives morning sun, which makes it a good morning wall in the winter, and afternoon wall in the summer. With a 5000' elevation, this is another year round area.

Access
Take Sunset Blvd west (Route 91) for 10.7 miles, through Santa Clara, to the Gunlock turn-off in the Shivwits Indian Reservation. Bear left at the Gunlock turn (hit your trip meter) and travel west for 8.5 miles. Turn left onto a gravel road crossing a yellow cattle guard, and continue another 1.9 miles to an intersection. Turn left and follow the gravel road for 0.7 mile (passing the Simian parking), drop down through a narrow wash. Park in the meadow just beyond. Walk up (east) the 4WD road for 0.3 mile to the far right of the formation and locate the trail to the base of the biggest buttress.

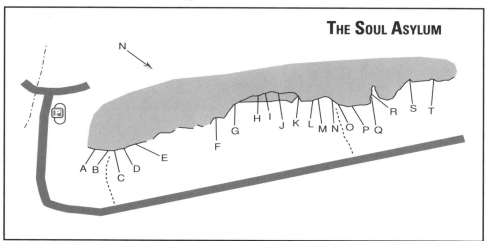

THE SOUL ASYLUM

THE SOUL ASYLUM

A. Happy Happy 5.9*
> *L. Jefferies*
> Friction slab past five bolts to a single bolt anchor (40' — or continue up and use tree for anchor).

B. Happy Helmet 5.11d**
> *K. Oldrid, M. Call*
> Short and sustained route on pockets and edges. Four bolts. (40')

C. Ren and Stimpy 5.11a*
> *K. Oldrid, M. Call*
> Nice variety of edges and pockets. Four bolts to chains. (40')

D. You Idiot 5.10d**
> *L. Jefferies*
> Short and fingery. Three bolts to chains. (35')

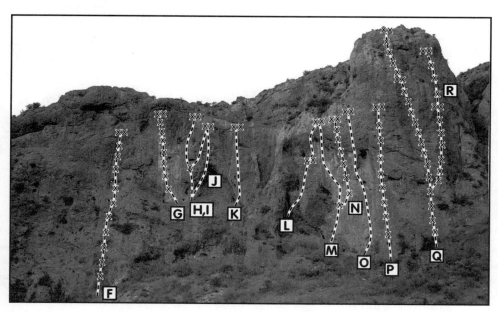

E. Joy! Joy! 5.9*
> *L. Jefferies*
> Friction slab to nice pockets. Three bolts to chains. (35')

F. Soul Train 5.11d/12a**
> *D. Biniaz, T. Goss*
> Edges on slab leads to steep pocketed face. Ten bolts to rap anchors. (85')

G. Lost Soul 5.12c***

L. Logston

Steep and technical on edges and pockets up beautiful white limestone. Seven bolts to anchor. (75')

H. White Soul Power 5.12a***

L. Jefferies

Steep climbing on smooth huecos to pockets in headwall. Ten bolts to chains. (70')

I. Pain Drops 5.12b**

T. Roberts

Shares first five bolts of H then right through steep rock. Nine bolts to chains. (60')

J. Flesh and Blood 5.13a**

T. Goss, D. Biniaz

Crawl up through center of cave past eight bolts to shared anchor. (60')

K. Wanagi (Ghost) 5.11d/12a*

L. Logston

Steep reachy start to technical moves above. Seven bolts to chains. (60')

L. Secrets and Lies 5.11a**

D. Biniaz, T. Goss

A nice warm-up. From the loose alcove, traverse right up sharp pockets to rap anchor in mid-wall, below alcove. (70')

Note: Continuation to top anchors is 5.12d.

M. Vision Seeker 5.12b***

L. Logston

Nice huecos to sequential crux, and steep moves out of pod. Ten bolts to chains. (80')

N. One Taste 5.12b***

D. Biniaz, T. Goss

Begin as for M and depart to right after fifth bolt. Climbs nice pockets through pod and bulge to rap anchor. Nine bolts. (70')

O. Project

P. Nine Lives 5.11b

N. McCullough

Pockets and sidepulls to committing crux. Eight bolts to chains. (75')

Q. Redcloud 5.10a**

J. Baldwin

Pocketed slab up face to top of formation. Seventeen bolts long. (160')

Note: 140' pitch. Midstation anchor allows the use of one 50m rope.

R. Blood Drive 5.10c**

T. Goss, D. Biniaz

Shares the first four bolts of Q then heads straight up through water-scoop on sculpted holds to a rap anchor. Fourteen bolts in 140'. A midway rap anchor at scoop allows for a descent with one rope. The route is 5.8 to this anchor.

S. Orion 5.10b/c***

J. Baldwin

From tree filled alcove, this is the left hand of two routes up gorgeous pockets and pinches. Nine bolts to rap anchor. (80')

T. Petrified 5.10c/d***

J. Baldwin

Right route stems up alcove then onto face with pinches and pockets to shared rap anchor. Nine bolts. (80')

U. Afterlife 5.10a***

L. Logston

If there's pockets like this in the afterlife sign me up. Six bolts to chains. (60')

V. Spirit World 5.9***

L. Logston

Six bolts lead past pockets so nice you won't want to let go of them. (60')

Gordon Lawson on Sweet Ennui (5.10a)
The Diamond

THE DIAMOND

The amount of exposed rock in the Utah Hills is often hard to fathom. Fins and ridges of limestone line the road like rows of sharks teeth waiting to bite into the heart and soles of unsuspecting climbers. Massive blocks hide in the pinon pines and smooth boulders lurk in canyon bottoms awaiting a chalked hand and slippered foot. Yet rising from this bounty of stone the Diamond dominates the landscape like a crown jewel surrounded by chips and splinters.

Though admired by numerous aspiring pioneers during the years when the more accessible walls were being developed, the brutal condition of the access road, and the subsequent approach kept potential suitors focused elsewhere. In 1995 the prolific Mike Tupper bolted the first route on lead – while wearing a backpack and approach shoes! This got the attention of several Salt Lake City climbers who began picking gems of their own.

By 1997 Lange Jefferies, Jeff Baldwin, Lee Logston, and Tim Roberts made the five hour drive every weekend loaded with bolts, batteries, and motivation. Like bolting postal employees, neither rain, nor sleet, nor hail, could deter these maniacs from delivering their appointed bolts; and soon the routes on the right side of the wall were equipped. With some multi-pitch projects well underway on the steep left side of the wall, The Diamond has much to offer those willing to brave the approach.

Season
The Diamond faces west-northwest, and receives afternoon sun and morning shade. The wall is at 6000' and is climbable all year.

Access
Follow the same directions for the Gorilla Cliffs, but continue past the parking area at the Simian Complex for 0.3 mile. Turn onto the second dirt road on the right.

4WD: Drive up the progressively steeper and rougher road and park at the mineshaft. Caution! This approach requires some skillful maneuvering on steep and rough roads with fatal dropoffs.

2WD: Park at the Soul Asylum parking and walk up the road to the mineshaft. Locate the trail which passes in front of the mine and follow the steep trail to the wall.

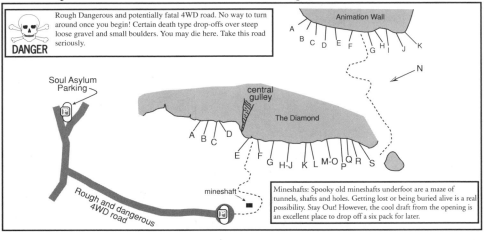

DANGER — Rough Dangerous and potentially fatal 4WD road. No way to turn around once you begin! Certain death type drop-offs over steep loose gravel and small boulders. You may die here. Take this road seriously.

Animation Wall

A B C D E F G H I J K N

Soul Asylum Parking

central gulley

The Diamond

A B C D E F G H-J K L M-O P Q R S

mineshaft

Mineshafts: Spooky old mineshafts underfoot are a maze of tunnels, shafts and holes. Getting lost or being buried alive is a real possibility. Stay Out! However, the cool draft from the opening is an excellent place to drop off a six pack for later.

Rough and dangerous 4WD road

THE DIAMOND

A. Project

B. Project

C. Project

D. Project

E. Diamond Joe 5.11d/12a*

J. Stone

To the right of the central buttress, climb pockets and edges past eight bolts moving rightwards to chains. (80')

F. Hope 5.13a***

L. Logston

Brilliant stone! Wonderful features on this long testpiece with fourteen bolts to chains. (120')

G. Flawless 5.12a***

T. Roberts

Vertical to slightly overhanging route weaves between wonderful variety of features. Nine bolts to chains. (85')

H. Crystalline Entity 5.12a***

L. Jefferies, L. Logston

Pockets and edges through steep scoop on positive holds eight bolts to common anchor. (80')

I. Brilliance 5.12c***

L. Jefferies, T. Roberts

Steep edging to reachy crux on tricky underclings. Eight bolts to common anchor. (80')

J. Diamonds are Forever 5.11c/d***

T. Roberts

Positive pockets lead to thin edges. Nine bolts to common anchor. (80')

K. Sweet Ennui 5.10b***

E. Tupper, M. Tupper

Some of the best pockets ever. Eight bolts, shares anchor with L. (80')

L. Pack Man 5.9**

M. Tupper, E. Tupper

First route on the crag. Move up flake to committing slab moves. Eight bolts to common anchor with K. (80')

M. Cullinan 5.10b**

J. Baldwin

From small cave climb up pocketed slab past 8 bolts to chains. (85')

N. Champagne 5.10a**

J. Baldwin

Ten feet right of M. Friction slab to shallow dihedral then left to the last three bolts of M. Shares anchor with M. (85')

O. Pink Panther 5.10b**

J. Baldwin

Shares start of N, then departs right to chains. Eight bolts. (80')

P. Clarity 5.10c***

L. Jefferies

Steep slab on thin edges and pure friction. Ten bolts to chains. (80')

Note: The second pitch is a project.

Q. Girl's Best Friend 5.10a**

L. Jefferies

Friction slab on edges, pockets, bulges and a small roof. Eight bolts to chains. (80')

R. Sell the Ring 5.11b**

L. Jefferies

Friction slab on small edges and pockets. Eight bolts to chains. (75')

S. Coal and Time 5.11a**

L. Jefferies

On the far right, a thin edging problem on an immaculate steep slab. Seven bolts to chains. (65')

Darl Biniaz on Clarity (5.10c)

THE ANIMATION WALL

In 1996 while hiking to the top of The Diamond to bolt a new climb, Lange Jefferies spotted the Animation Wall sitting on the other side of a talus slope.

Enchanted by both the secluded setting, and bullet proof tiers of overhanging limestone, Jefferies enlisted the help of several friends in the arduous task of equipping this remote wall. With major contributions by the prolific Jeff Baldwin, this wall sports a range of routes sure to compensate for what may only be described as a burly approach by southern Utah standards.

Season

Spring, winter, and fall are the prime seasons to be in the Utah Hills. This wall faces west-northwest and goes into the sun in the afternoon. The wall is at 6300'.

Access

Follow the approach to The Diamond. Turn right onto the cragside trail and walk southwest around the right side of The Diamond. Follow the trail up to and across the talus slope to The Animation Wall on the far side of the talus. This is about an additional 300 yards from The Diamond.

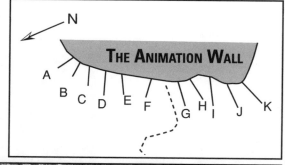

THE ANIMATION WALL

A. Itchy 5.9*
L. Jefferies
Edgy slab on well featured gray stone. Six bolts to rap anchors. (55')

B. Scratchy 5.10a**
L. Jefferies
Sharp crimps on bulletproof limestone. Six bolts to rap anchor. (55')

C. Flaming Mo 5.12b/c***
L. Jefferies
Sidepull through overhang onto slab. Seven bolts to rap anchor. (60')

D. Project

E. Blade 5.12d**
J. Baldwin, L. Jerreries
Through beautiful overhanging tiers onto slab. Seven bolts to rap anchor. (60')

F. Cracklin Wallnuts 5.12c***
J. Baldwin, L. Jefferies
Nice pockets to roof, up steep sidepulls to a final slab. Seven bolts to rap anchor. (60')

G. Project

H. Project

I. Brotha Smurf 5.11a*
L. Jefferies
Steep gray slab with somewhat sharp but nice edges. Six bolts to rap anchor. (50')

J. Smurf 5.11a*
L. Jefferies
10' right of I. Six bolts to rap anchors. (55')

K. Blank's Plank 5.10b*
L. Jefferies
Similar to the routes on the left but lower angle and nicer holds. Six bolts to rap anchor. (55')

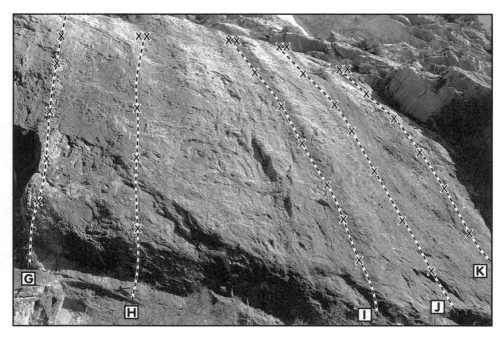

JB's Crag

This nice piece of rock is just a couple of minutes hike off the approach road to The Soul Asylum, and offers three routes on solid stone with very reasonable grades. Developed by Jeff Baldwin, these routes are a nice change from the steep pumpfests typical of many limestone areas, and a tribute to Jeff's vision and generosity in bolting climbs that are within the reach of the average sport climber.

Season

JB's Crag faces northeast and receives little or no sun in the winter, and afternoon shade in summer. The wall is at 5000'.

Access

Approach as for The Soul Asylum, and turn right off the approach road just prior to the left turn. The wall is on the backside of the ridge coming down on the right.

JB's Crag

A. Full Moon Rising 5.10a**
J. Baldwin
Through small roof then past six bolts to common anchor. (70')

B. Mist and Shadows 5.11b*
J. Baldwin
Straight up steep gray slab on crimps and edges. Seven bolts to common anchor. (75')

C. Stonecrab 5.11b**
J. Baldwin
No need to be crabby on stone this nice. Edges and crimps on friction face. Seven bolts to common anchor. (75')

THE BOY WALL

Exploration in the Utah Hills is very convenient because mining roads offer access to areas which would normally require many calories worth of thrashing about. Lee Logston and Brian Mecham took advantage of a relatively easy approach to develop this small wall up a hidden canyon behind a prominent ridge. The routes are sustained pocket and edge affairs up compact streaked limestone in an isolated and forested little canyon.

Season

At 5500' with a southwest aspect. Spring, fall, and winter are best times to visit this little crag.

Access

Follow Soul Asylum directions. Walk up the very rocky road, as per Soul Asylum, but depart right after 50 yards and follow a good dirt road for 0.25 mile. Bear right at an obvious intersection and at the apex of a hill look left into the wood for this 35' high wall.

Note: This 30 minute approach may seem like a long way to go to do three routes. But if you're into solitude or exploring, this crag may be up your alley.

THE BOY WALL

A. Future Boy 5.12c**

L. Logston

Crimps and pockets through a bulge with a nasty looking sloper sidepull. Three bolts to chains. (30')

B. Sport Boy 5.11d/12a**

L. Logston

Edges, pockets and sidepulls to a steep bulge. Pull through on big holds to chains. Three bolts. (30')

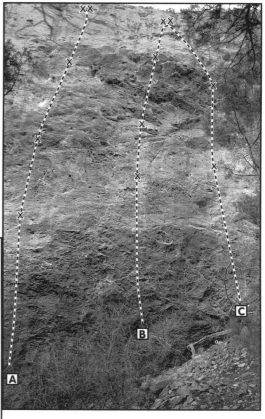

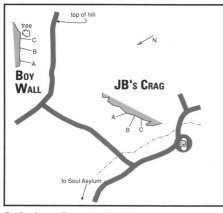

C. Asthma Boy 5.12b/c*

B. Mecham

Hard to catch your breath on moves like these. Reachy crimps through bulge to B's anchor. Stick clip first bolt, two bolts total to anchor. (30')

THE WARM-UP WALL

Nearly forgotten in an obscure corner of the Utah Hills, the Warm-Up Wall is another small crag where one is sure to find absolute solitude on even the busiest of climbing weekends. Cryptically described in an old issue of Rock & Ice, the first ascent data has been lost to posterity, yet the routes here remain a testament to somebody's eye for a nice line or two.

Season

Most summer days maybe too hot for this crag as it receives morning sun. Spring, fall and winter are best for this 5000' elevation cliff.

Access

Follow directions as per Gorilla Cliffs. Just prior to intersection at 1.9miles, locate a dirt road on the right. Follow it west for 0.7 mile, approch as close as possible to the cliff and locate an adequate parking spot.

THE WARM-UP WALL

A. Tropical Depression 5.10a*

FA unknown

A smooth bronze streak of pockets and edges. Four bolts to a funky cable anchor. (50')

B. Temperate Zone 5.10c*

FA unknown

Nice pockets in a tan streak. Five bolts (including a glue-in ringbolt) to chains. (50')

C. Torrid Zone 5.12a*

FA unknown

Five bolts lead past edges and nice pockets in solid stone. Chain anchors. (50')

D. Hot Blooded 5.12a*

FA unknown

Beautiful beige streak to gray headwall. Six bolts to chains. (60')

E. The Better Edge 5.12b*

FA unknown

Climb huecos past a ring bolt to streaked arete and rusty chains. Six bolts. (60')

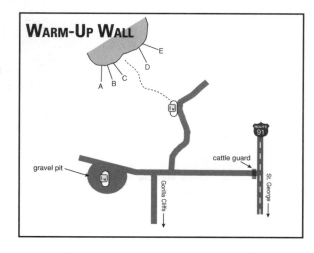

WELCOME SPRINGS

Michael Nad on Worshipping the Limestone Gods (5.11b)

WELCOME SPRINGS

With much of the focus on the area around Gorilla Cliffs and Black and Tan, the north side of old Highway 91 was somewhat ignored until Shane Willet took a good look at the Welcome Springs drainage in the winter of 1994.

Willet began bolting on the Sumo Wall, and returned to Salt Lake City with tales of limestone walls that went on forever. Several of Willet's friends subsequently put up routes on the Wailing Wall yet inexplicably left the Cathedral untouched.

In May of 1995 local climbers Todd Goss and Michael Nad began route development in the Cathedral with Natural Born Drillers. Between stints of lead bolting, the pair would de-stress with the occasional route on the Sumo Wall, eventually filling in the wall to the right of the cave. Mike Tupper added Dragonseed to the steep left side in '96 as well as some futuristic projects through the steepest central part of the wall. The Wailing Wall received renewed attention by Goss in '97 and '98 with several new routes completed.

Season

Year round area at 5000'. Summer climbing in the Cathedral and Wailing Wall is possible virtually all day as both crags face true north with late afternoon sunlight falling on the Wailing Wall around 5:00 p.m. Both walls can be too cold on some winter days though tolerable on most. The Sumo Wall receives sun until early afternoon in the summer, and limited sun in the morning in the winter.

Access

Follow Sunset Blvd. out of St. George for 10.7 miles to the Gunlock turnoff and bear left (hit your trip meter). After continuing 11.6 miles on Route 91, a graffiti covered cliff will be visible on the left side of the road. Just past this cliff is a gravel road marked High Desert Game Ranch. Take this 2WD road for 2.0 miles to another gravel road on the right (BLM sign for Welcome Springs) Follow this road for 2.0 miles to a wash and park. Walk up the wash to the south, bearing left at the big cottonwood tree, and the Sumo Wall will come into view on the left after 0.5 mile. Another 0.5 mile will bring you to the Cathedral Trail on the right, the trailhead of which is marked with cairns in the wash. Climb this steep trail to the Cathedral or bear right to the Wailing Wall. With 4WD it is possible to drive up the wash to the trailhead. Please stay on the trail, the area around the Cathedral has delicate and beautiful plant life.

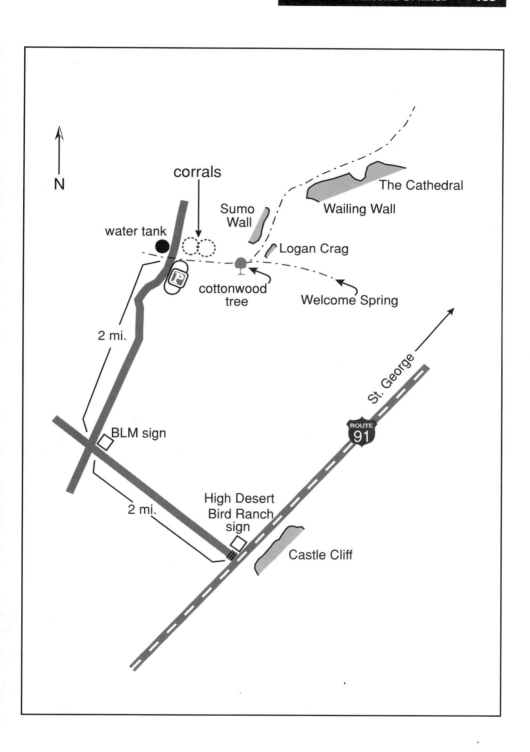

THE LOGAN CRAG

This wall is the first formation encountered on the right, about 0.25 mile up the wash. The wall is about 20' from the trail. Routes are listed left to right.

A. Andy's Route 5.11a*

A. Ross

Sharp edges up compact gray stone. Four bolts to anchors. (50')

B. Jim's Route 5.10d*

J. Howe

Crimps and sidepulls with an occasional pocket.
Four bolts to chains. (50')

THE SUMO WALL

A. Project

B. Dragonseed 5.13b**

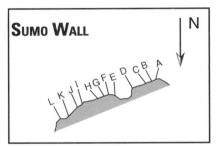

M. Tupper

Steep and reachy crimping on great rock. Seven bolts to coldshuts. (60')

C. Project

D. Project

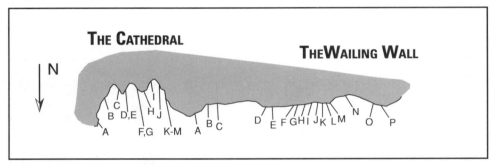

E. Picking Sumo's Nose 5.12b*

M. Nad, S. Willet

From right side of cave climb rail and pockets to nostril, then reachy moves gain ledge and easy climbing to chains. Six bolts. (60')

F. Falling Bats 5.11c**

S. Willet

Shallow dihedral on edges then straight up vertical face to chains. Eleven bolts. (85' – use caution when lowering!).

G. Too Fat For A Sleeping Bag 5.11d***

M. Nad, T. Goss

Same start as F, then right through budge up thin edging. Shares one bolt with H up high and crosses right to its own anchors. Twelve bolts total to rap anchor. (85')

H. Love Handles 5.11d*

M. Nad, T. Goss

Thin edging and crimping on sharp rock. Ten bolts to rap anchor. (85')

I. Geisha Knife Fight 5.10d***

T. Goss, M. Nad

Super pockets to bulge and big edges to top. Seven bolts to rap anchor. (75')

J. Nipple Extractor 5.11a*

J. Smith, T. Goss

Technical moves through bulge. Shares two bolts with I and ends on I's anchor. Nine bolts. (75')

K. The Wasteland 5.8*

S. Willet

Tricky slab moves lead to enjoyable pockets. Ten bolts to chains. (80')

L. Cheeks of Chong 5.9**

A. Hughes, T. Goss

Another bulge thing to easier climbing. Six bolts to rap anchor. (65')

THE CATHEDRAL

Access

Continue North up wash/road past Sumo Wall for 0.5 mile. The Cathedral Cave will become visible on the ridge to your right. Locate a trail marked with cairns in the wash.

A. Idol Worship 5.11c**

M. Nad, T. Goss

Good edges through overhang lead to big holds on sharp slab. Seven bolts to chains. (50')

B. Raising Cain 5.12b***

T. Goss, D. Biniaz

Eight bolts through super pockets. (70')

C. Holy Shit 5.12a*

M. Nad, J. Nad

Nice face climbing on positive holds leads to bulge and birdshit- covered holds. Five bolts to coldshuts. (50')

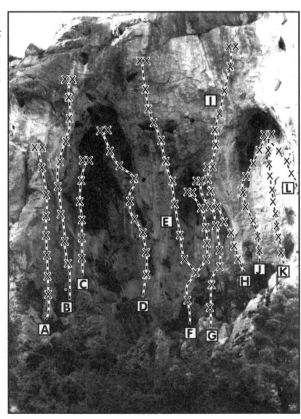

Michal Nad on Thar She Blows (5.10d)

D. Worshipping the Limestone Gods 5.11b***
T. Goss, M. Nad
Steep, pumpy jugfest, with the best holds hard to find. Eight bolts to rap anchor. (60')

E. Project

F. Pagan Rituals 5.10b***
T. Goss, M. Nad
Edges, pockets, threads, tufa pinches and bat shit. This route has it all. Seven bolts to rap anchor. (60')

G. Sacrilege 5.11d**
T. Goss, S. Platt
Bouldery start to slab pockts and a hard finish through six bolts. (60')

H. The Epiphany 5.11d**
T. Goss, P. Lowe
Up blunt arete to hueco, then hard pockets to rap anchor. Seven bolts. (65')

I. Project (open)

J. Space Shuttle to Kolob 5.13a***
T. Perkins
Steep pockets to bouldery crux. Eight bolts to common anchor. (65')

K. Project

L. Speaking in Tounges 5.12b***
M. Nad, T. Goss
Bouldery start leads to sustained pockets and edges to common anchor. Nine bolts. (65')

M. Natural Born Drillers 5.12c***
M. Nad, T. Goss
First route in the Cathedral. Great pockets and smooth edges past chains (to reduce rope drag, clip chain then unclip after clipping the next bolt) through bat cave to final headwall. Sixteen bolts to rap anchor. (85'– even with a 60m rope. Be sure to clip the chain on the descent).

N. Project

O. Latter Day Sinners 5.13b**
M. Nad, J. Nad
Steep and reachy past six bolts to mid-route chains on route M. (65')

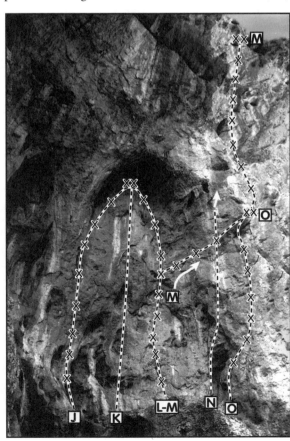

THE WAILING WALL

A. Harpooned 5.12b*
J. Woodward
Sharp edges to friction crux. Nine bolts and slung thread to anchor. (80')

B. Project

C. Baleen 5.12c
FA unknown
Edges and pockets in a well-featured wall. Eight bolts to anchor. (80')

D. The Infidels 5.13a***
T. Goss, E. Jones
Slab to boulder problem, then nice edges to thin finish on beautiful white crimps. Eight bolts to rap anchor. (75')

E. Project

F. Rising Expectations 5.11d***
T. Goss, R. Fisher
Nice edges to rising traverse on awesome pockets. Eight bolts to rap anchor. (75')

G. Mobey 5.12
FA unknown
Shares start with F then straight up on nice edges. At press time the hangers had been removed on this route. (80')

H. Project

I. Call Me Ishmael 5.12d
FA unknown
Sharp edges on just over vertical wall. Eight bolts to anchor (long run-out at 6th bolt!). (80')

J. Casting Aspersions 5.11b***
T. Goss, D. Biniaz
Slab to short overhang to stemming corner. Ten bolts to rap anchor. (80')

K. Cap'n Ahab 5.11d**
FA unknown
Steep pockets and edges to awkward traverse at top. Seven bolts to rap anchor. (70')

L. Heretic Wisdom 5.12a***
M. Nad, T. Goss
Wonderful arete with great moves. Nine bolts to rap anchor. (65')

M. Project

N. Project

O. The White Whale 5.11b
FA unknown
Left traverse on very sharp rock past four bolts to chains. (50')

P. Thar She Blows 5.10d
FA unknown
Sharp pockets on a slab. Four bolts to anchor. (50')

WOODBURY ROAD CRAGS

Bo Beck on K-6 at Kelly's Rock (5.11b)

THE WOODBURY ROAD CRAGS

Cresting the top of Utah Hill and starting the long descent to the Virgin River at Littlefield, the landscape changes from the Great Basin ecosystem to the Mojave in just a few short miles. Pinon and juniper suddenly give way to Joshua Trees, as the slopes of the Beaver Dam Mountains ever so slowly tumble west toward Beaver Dam Wash. About halfway to the river, a dirt road comes in on the left and offers an interesting loop drive through these stunning desert mountains.

The beginning of this loop road is the site of the Woodbury Desert Study Area, where scientific studies on desert flora and fauna are performed. Of perhaps greater interest to rock climbers, are the studies of geology being performed on some of the brilliant limestone crags in this area.

Developed over several years by Kelly Oldrid, Boone Speed, Tim Wagner, Geoff Weigand, Jeff Pederson, and others the crags in this area offer a bountiful variety of climbing styles and grades.

Climbing stone this nice, in an area as pristine and lovely as this, seems too good to be true. This could in fact be the case if users of this area don't act responsibly and accordingly in this sensitive area. Reflecting the necessity for us to keep our impact to an absolute minimum, the untrampled landscape east of the road has been proposed for wilderness designation.

Season

Both crags in this area are predominately winter, spring and fall areas. Summer climbing is possible, but not pleasant especially in the afternoon. Black and Tan Wall faces east-northeast and Kelly's Rock faces north-northwest. Both walls are at 3200'.

Access

From Bluff St. turn west onto Sunset Blvd. and drive 10.7 miles west through the town of Santa Clara, to the Gunlock turnoff. Hit trip meter and bear left at the intersection and travel west for 14.4 miles to a gravel road on the left. There is a brown BLM sign indicating "Woodbury Desert Study Area". Turn left onto this road and travel 3.2 miles (2WD). The Black and Tan Wall will appear on the right. Park in the turnoff and locate the trail to the center of the wall. To get to Kelly's Rock walk back down the road 100 yards to the cattleguard and turn right up the wash for 300 yards. The wall is on the right.

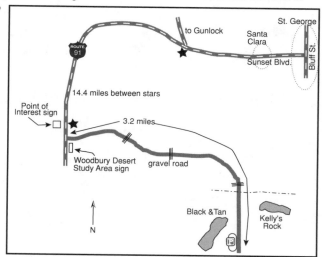

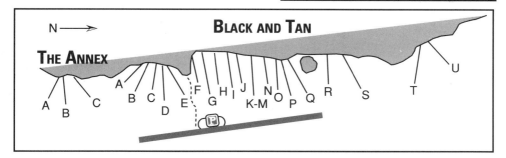

BLACK AND TAN

A. Campus Boy 5.13c*
C. Hadley
Boulder problem start to sidepulls and crimps up white streak. Five bolts to chains. (50')

B. Dickheads 5.12d***
B. Speed
Beautiful route but hard start, then wonderful pockets. Long, but easy runout to anchor. Four bolts to chains. (50')

C. Da Riddler 5.12a**
B. Speed
Great pockets and sidepulls on steep streaked rock. Four bolts to common anchor. (50')

D. Dull Boy 5.11d*
B. Speed, T. Wagner
Blocky edges and pinches tending left to common anchor. Four bolts. (50')

E. Bed Head 5.11c*
T. Wagner, B. Speed
Blocky start moving right into short corner, small roof and finish on slab. Four bolts to chains. (50')

F. Smoking Drum 5.13a/b**
J. Pederson
Big moves on flakes through roof, then edges and pockets on headwall. Eight bolts to sport anchor. (55')

G. Talking Smack 5.13c**
J. Pederson
From the back of cave horizontal climbing for 30 feet on flakes leads to edgy wall above. Eight bolts to sport anchor. (55')

H. Project
I. Project
J. Project

K. Sniffing Glue 5.13d**
G. Weigand, J. Pederson
Common start through roof on flakes and crimps then left up pocketed and streaked wall past hueco to chains. Seven bolts. (55')

L. Shooting Horse 5.13c**

G. Weigand, J. Pederson

Shares first two bolts of K then up past two more through shallow dihedral and small roof then back left to join K. Six bolts. (55')

M. Project

N. Minus Five 5.13a**

G. Weigand

On right edge of cave, climb flakes to crimps past three bolts to chains on large ledge. (50')

O. Shades of Grey 5.11b**

FA unknown

Pockets and sidepulls on solid streaked rock. Five bolts to chains. (45')

P. Jumanji 5.12a**

FA unknown

Above cave, excellent pockets to crimpy crux. Five bolts to coldshuts. (45')

Q. Razorblade Suitcase 5.12d*

FA unknown

Just to the left of the block, sharp edges lead left past four bolts to chains. (40')

R. Look Sharp 5.11d*

FA unknown

20' right of the block, pockets and sharp sidepulls trending left past four bolts to chains. (40')

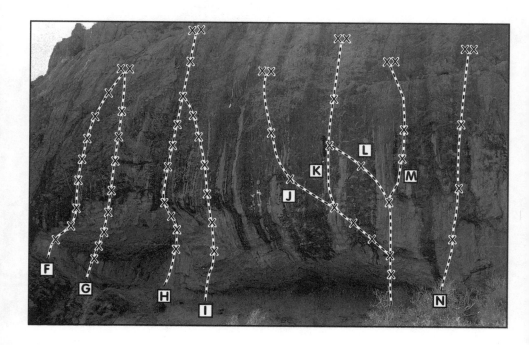

Note: The area around Drunken Speed Fisherman has a raptor nest site which has been active in the recent past. Please climb in another area if the nest is occupied.

S. Drunken Speed Fisherman 5.10b**
> *FA unknown*
> Just right of Look Sharp. Tan and gold streaks with big edges. Six bolts to chains. (50')

T. Tickman 5.11b**
> *M. Nad, T. Goss*
> Gold-streaked face with pockets and edges past four bolts to rap anchor. (45')

U. Pangs of Ignorance 5.11a**
> *T. Goss, M. Nad*
> Sharp crimping and pockets right of T. Shares rap anchor. Four bolts. (45')

BLACK AND TAN – THE ANNEX

Access
When the access trail meets the wall, turn and walk left along the cliff.

A. Clean Sweep 5.11b*
> *T. Wagner, B. Speed*
> Tan edges to sharp crimps in bronze streak. Three bolts (runout) to chains. (45')

B. The Prying Game 5.10b
> *T. Wagner, B. Speed*
> Short route up nice orange streaks. Three bolts to chains. (40')

C. Block Party 5.10a
> *T. Wagner, B. Speed*
> Diagonal gray streak on edges and sidepulls. Four bolts to common anchor. (50')

Jeff Pederson on a project at the Black and Tan Wall

KELLY'S ROCK

A. K-1 5.10a*

B. Mecham

Huge and pointy holds in water runnels lead to small scoop, more sharp holds to rap anchor. Two bolts. (40')

B. K-2 5.8*

J. Baldwin

Similar to A. Big and sharp holds on slab past two bolts to anchor. Stick clip recommended. (40')

C. K-3 5.9*

K. Oldrid

To right of a corner climb nice positive holds past three bolts to chains. (40')

D. K-4 5.11b*

K. Oldrid

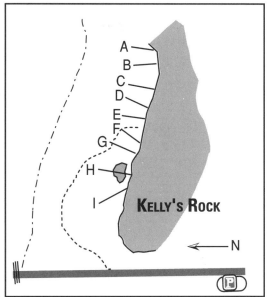

Edges in overlaps lead to smooth slab easily climbed on the left but more difficult staying on the bolt line. Four bolts to chains. (50')

Note: There is a 5.9 variation that climbs to the left of the bolts.

E. K-5 5.10b**

K. Oldrid

Slabby overlaps to tricky face, through small roof and scoop to chains. Four bolts. First bolt very high! (50')

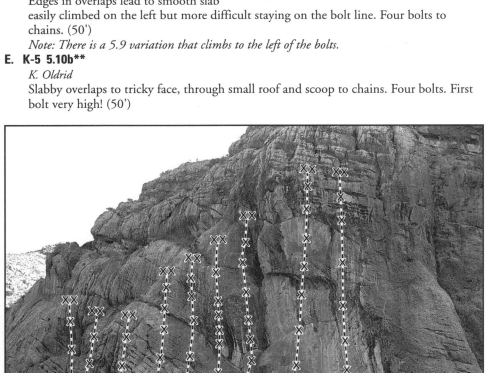

F. K-6 5.11b***

K. Oldrid

Stepped slab to wonderful overhanging scoop with great features. Six bolts to chains. (50')

G. K-7 5.12d*

K. Oldrid

Slab to steep pocketed face and diagonal seam. Then up steep friction slab to chains in hueco. Seven bolts. (55')

H. K-8 5.11b***

K. Oldrid

One of the best routes in Utah. Beautiful pockets and edges through two small roofs. Excellent stone, great route! Seven bolts to chains. (60')

I. K-9 5.12b*

K. Oldrid

Nice smooth tan rock with somewhat obscure features. Six bolts to chains. (55')

Chris Cluff on Drunken Speed Fisherman (5.10b).

VIRGIN RIVER GORGE

Chris Sharma on Necessary Evil (5.14c)   Jim Thornburg photo

THE VIRGIN RIVER GORGE (VRG)

The Virgin River Gorge was once a peaceful place where the only rock climbers were the desert bighorn sheep scrambling up the exposed faces and gullies of the Beaver Dam mountains. The hiss and gurgle of the Virgin River slowly cutting through the resilient rock was all that could be heard in this remote and austere piece of desert. Twelve years of blasting and demolition changed all that, and with the opening of Interstate 15, the only hiss now heard in the gorge is that of tires on asphalt. Though climbers from all over the country had been passing by the limestone walls of the VRG ever since I-15 was opened, it took visionaries like Boone Speed, Jeff Pederson, Randy Leavitt, Tom Gilje, Scott Frye and others to recognize the opportunities the VRG offered. Routes of every character and style imaginable are represented here – from long and technical, to short and thuggish. This impeccable streaked limestone offers a climber's wish list of features to pull on.

While the climbing itself is brilliant, the factory-like atmosphere is clearly not conducive to reflection or relaxation. No climber comes here with any intention other than to pull as hard as they can and leave when they are done. As one of the greatest concentrations of hard routes in the region, the VRG will certainly not fail to offer most climbers the challenge they are looking for.

Season

The VRG is at 2000'. Summers are out of the question. Winter, early spring and late fall are the best times to visit.

Access

From St. George travel south on I-15 for 25.0 miles. After mile marker 14, slow down and get in the right lane. Just after the raised roadway bridge, turn right off the roadway onto a gravel parking area. Get well off the road, and use extreme caution entering or exiting traffic. When reversing direction on the interstate use the nearest exit and not the median strip turnarounds; this is illegal and gives us a bad name with the authorities.

"You're obliged to pretend respect for people and institutions you think absurd. You live attached in a cowardly fashion to moral and social conventions you despise, condemn, and know lack all foundation. It is that permanent contradiction between your ideas and desires, and all the dead formalities and vain pretenses of your civilization which makes you sad, troubled, and unbalanced." - Octave Mirbeau

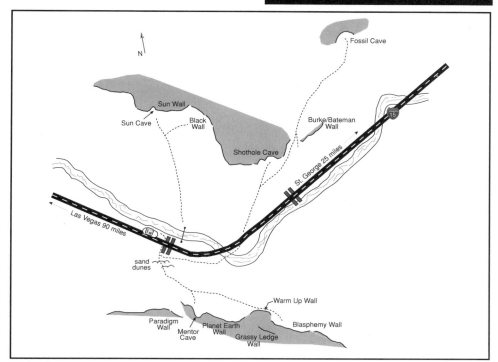

THE BLASPHEMY WALL

Access

Park on southbound pull-out and cross under bridge turning left at other end. Follow trail across sand dunes and up to wall. Bear left at intersection and pass the Warm-Up Wall. The Blasphemy Wall is the obviously streaked bulging wall on the right.

A. I Saw Jesus at the Chains 5.13a*

L. Bateman, G. Burke

On small platform in oblong cave, big positive holds lead through roof to crimping on streaked face. Fifteen bolts to chains. (100')

B. Sins of the Flesh 5.12c*

D. Goolsby

Shares start of C, departs left at third bolt, and launches up dark streak with wonderful pockets to coldshuts. Ten bolts. (90')

C. Hi Flames Drifter 5.12c*

B. Boyle

Beautiful smooth pockets to edges in streaked wall. Six bolts to chains halfway up wall. (80')

D. Bogus Pedophile Charge 5.12c*

T. Wagner

Some may want to do this one for the route name alone. Continue up natural line of holds above the anchors on C through pod to chains. Thirteen bolts. (115')

E. Fall of Man 5.13b***

B. Speed

One of the first routes and one of the best. Sinker pockets to dark streak with pockets and small crimps. Runout to thirteenth bolt makes the route name applicable. Fifteen bolts to chains. (125')

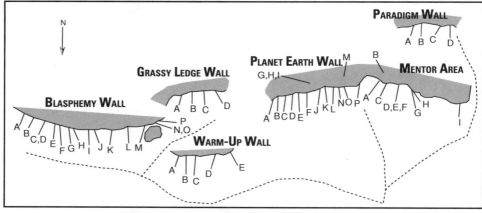

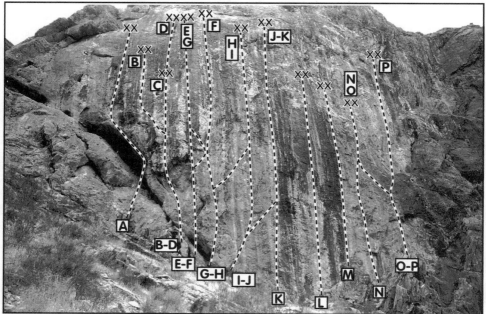

F. Dark Boy 5.13b**

J. Pederson

Departs E at fourth bolt then right up steel gray stone on underclings and small edges to seventh bolt. Easier climbing leads to chains. Eleven bolts. (120')

G. F-Dude 5.14a***

B. Speed

A link-up involving the crux sections of Dude, Dark Boy, and Fall of Man. Fourteen bolts to the chains on E. (125')

H. Dude 5.13c***

S. Frye

Pockets, crimps and body-tension sidepulls. Twelve bolts to chains. (85')

I. Don't Call Me Dude 5.13c***

S. Frye

Diagonal line of pockets leads to crimps, edges, pockets and pinches. Eleven bolts to shared anchor. (85')

J. The Route of All Evil 5.14a***

B. Speed

Shares first three bolts of I then crimp up sustained bulging streaked wall on small pockets and edges. Eleven bolts to chains. (90')

K. Necessary Evil 5.14c***

C. Sharma

Direct start to route J through extreme crimps on tiny edges. Eleven bolts to chains. (90')

L. Project
M. Don't Call Me Coach 5.13d*

FA unknown

Knobby pinches to edges in tan streak. Ten bolts to chains. (75')

N. Swear to God 5.13b*

T. Wagner

Small crimps and pockets through bulge to finish on O. Ten bolts. (75')

O. Bloody Mary 5.11c**

T. Wagner, B. Speed

Pockets and edges through small roof then easier ground and shared chains. Ten bolts. (75')

P. Erotic Jesus 5.13a**

T. Wagner

Shares first five bolts of O then right up streaked wall of blocky edges to chains. Ten bolts. (100')

THE GRASSY LEDGE WALL

Access

From right side of The Blasphemy Wall scramble up boulders 30' to the base of the wall.

A. Dead on the Phone 5.11d*

B. Folsom

Straight through the big huecos to thin edges. Six bolts to chains. (60')

B. Catalyst 5.11d**

G. Mayer

1st pitch: To right of huecos, climb beautiful streaked wall past five bolts to chains on big ledge. (60')

2nd pitch: From the ledge, eight bolts lead up smooth gray and tan wall on edges and sidepulls. Chain anchor. (70')

C. Bugger Bill 5.12b**

G. Burke, L. Bateman

Sharp edges and small pockets in bulletproof gray stone. Five bolts to chains. (60')

D. Shyster Myster 5.11d*

G. Burke, L. Bateman

Four bolts lead through sharp crimps in compact gray limestone. Chain anchor. (60')

THE WARM-UP WALL

Access

The trail to The Blasphemy Wall goes past this crag.

A. Smoked Chub 5.10b

P. Hodges

To the right of obvious huecos, nice edges in smooth stone. Four bolts to chains on ledge. (40')

B. Lyme Disease 5.10c*

B. Speed

You may get "lime" disease from climbing on limestone this nice. Three bolts to chains. (40')

C. Call Me Mike 5.11a*

M. Call

Through hueco to blunt arete right of the water trough. Four bolts to shared anchor with B. (40')

D. Spook 5.11c

J. Black

Thin edges through bulge to pockets and pinches above. Four bolts to chains. (40')

E. Corporate Slut 5.9*

C. Anker

Diagonal huecos and nice edges to bulge. Nice route for the grade. Five bolts to chains. (40')

Scott Frye on F-Dude (5.13c)

THE PLANET EARTH WALL

Access

Use the pullout on southbound turnout. Cross under bridge and turn left. Cross sand dunes and pick up a trail to the obvious cave.

A. Deliverance 5.13a
L. Anderson
Small edges and sidepulls on nice tan rock. Eight bolts to chains. (65')

B. Redneck 5.12b*
J. Visser
Flake to nice edges and reachy pockets. Seven bolts to A's chains. (65')

C. Joe Six Pack 5.13a***
R. Leavitt
Departs right of the fourth bolt of B. Pockets, edges and underclings lead through bulge to chains. Twelve bolts. (100')

D. Project

E. Horse Latitudes 5.14a***
R. Leavitt
Huecos and pockets lead to roof then bulging sustained streaked wall. Ten bolts to chains. (100')

F. Dirt Cowboy 5.12c**
R. Leavitt
Bouldery start leads to big holds through roof and technical headwall to chains. Eight bolts. (60')

G. Planet Earth 5.14a***
R. Leavitt
From top of F, straight up two bolts on edges, then left into pockets and slopers up bulging wall to chains. Fifteen bolts to chains. (100')

H. Captain Fantastic 5.13c***
R. Leavitt
From top of F, head straight up two bolts then move right to mono-thread, sustained crimpy sidepulls, dyno, and slopers to chains. Fourteen bolts. (100')

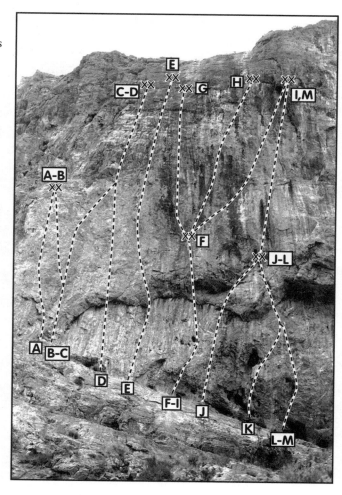

I. False Witness 5.13a*

R. Leavitt

From top of F, traverse right through sidepulls and crimps in concave face to M anchors. Seventeen bolts. (100')

J. Project

K. Don't Believe the Hype 5.12a**

S. Olmstead, C. Schneider

Large huecos lead to sequential sidepulls and roof to chains. Seven bolts. (45')

L. Surrender Dorothy 5.12d*

B. Speed

Hueco start leads to small and sequential crimping. Eight bolts to chains. (50')

M. Project

N. Hell Comes to Frogtown 5.13d*

F. Nicole

Drastic crimping in bulging blocky wall. Six bolts to chains. (35')

O. Quick Fixe 5.11d

L. Anderson

Big flake to reachy pocket. Five bolts to sport anchor. (40')

P. Sensory Overload 5.13b*

T. Yaniro

On left side of the cave, pockets lead to roof and edges to anchor. Fourteen bolts. (85')

MENTOR CAVE

A. Mentor 5.12b***

T. Gilje, D. Osman

Jugs, buckets, leg thread, mono, pockets, all on wonderfully steep rock. Likely the best route of the grade in the region. Nine bolts. (60')

B. Wowser 5.12d*

D. Welsh

Same as route A through roof then depart left past three bolts to Sensory Overload anchors. Thirteen bolts. (90')

C. Subterfuge 5.13a**

T. Gilje

Positive pockets lead to technical powerful sidepulls and wild roof moves to A's anchors. Eleven bolts. (60')

D. Bowser 5.12c**

S. Frye

Twenty-five feet right of C route. Follows diagonal line of huecos to roof and joins route A to anchors. Twelve bolts. (65')

E. Bowser Wowser 5.13a/b

S. Frye

Same start as D but continue left to Sensory Overload anchors, via sloping huecos and sinker pockets. Sixteen bolts. (100')

F. Mars 5.13b*

B. Speed

Same start as D then straight up at third bolt through desperate crimps and roof to chains. Eight bolts. (60')

G. Corrosion 5.12c**

B. Speed

Reachy crimps and slopers lead to small roof and crimpy slab finish. Eight bolts. (60')

H. Brutus 5.11b*

B. Speed

From small ledge route leads through huecos right to big holds and slab finish. Eight bolts to common anchor with G. (60')

I. Drop Chop 5.10d

FA unknown

On small pillar blocky holds and sharp pockets lead past seven bolts to chains. (50')

THE PARADIGM WALL

Access

To reach this obscure and little-visited crag follow the trail towards the Mentor Cave. Look for the wall up and right that requires a scramble.

A. Paradigm 5.12c*

B. Speed, B. Boyle

Thin and crimps edges up streaked wall to chains. Eight bolts. (60')

B. Velvet Overground 5.12c**

J. Pederson

Shares first bolt with A then up and right on edges and pinches. Eight bolts to chains. (60')

C. Dim 5.12c*

B. Speed

Sloping edges and reachy crimps past six bolts to chains. (60')

D. The Hunger 5.12d*

B. Speed

Need an appetite for crimpers on this. Seven bolts to chains. (60')

THE SUN CAVE

A. Relapse 5.13c**

B. Ohran

At the back of the cave follow eleven bolts up through thuggishness to chains. (50')

B. Scared Straight 5.13b**

J. Pederson

A direct finish to route C heading straight up to A's anchors. Ten bolts. (50')

C. Heroin 5.12d**

J. Pederson

Overhanging dihedral leads to big moves on underside of a roof moving right to chains. Ten bolts. (55')

D. Needle Me 5.13b/c**

J. Pederson

From the inside corner of the cave hard, steep climbing on pockets and flakes. Eight bolts. (40')

E. Small Dose 5.12a*

J. Pederson

Shares several bolts with F, then left onto the finish of D. Six bolts. (40')

F. Forever Man 5.12c***

B. Boyle

Great route up the longest part of the cave. It goes forever, man! Seventeen bolts to chains. Not all bolts shown on photo. (70')

G. Under a Sweltering Sky 5.11d*

M. Tupper

Not pictured. To start this route, you must first reach the anchors on F by either climbing that route or scrambling up slabs until it is possible to reach the anchors. After reaching the anchors, crawl like a fly along the roof towards the entrance and clip the chains on the face above. Seven bolts. (60')

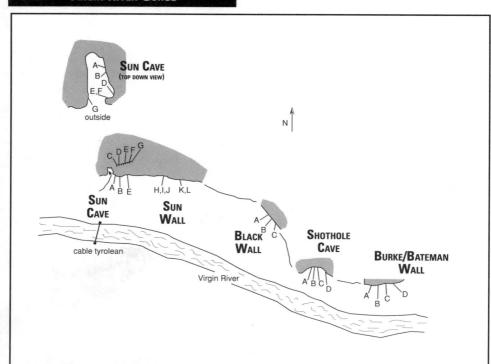

THE SUN WALL

A. Solar Eclipse 5.12a

FA unknown

Just outside the cave, blocky pinches and pockets through roof to common anchor on ledge. Eight bolts. (75')

B. Access 5.10d*

J. Pederson

Blocky pockets through roof to edges above. Eight bolts to common anchor on ledge. (75')

C. Helios 5.13c**

Bolted by J. Visser

Begin from the ledge. This route shares the first three bolts of D then heads left through the roof on excellent rock. Eight bolts to chains. (80')

D. Sundiver 5.13d***

Bolted by J. Pederson

Blocky pinches to overhang on sidepulls and edges then pocketed face with tufas to anchors. Fifteen bolts to chains. (85')

E. Truck Driver 5.13c**

R. Leavitt

1st pitch: Pinches up slab to chains on ledge. Seven bolts. (5.10b, 85')
2nd pitch: Blocky section leads to sustained headwall on sidepulls, underclings, pockets, and edges. Nine bolts to chains. (5.13c, 90')

F. Sunstroke 5.13c

Bolted by M. Tupper

Blocky edges to pockets and underclings through final bulge to chains on ledge. Eleven bolts. (85')

G. Sunchipped 5.12c
Bolted by T. White
Big edges and pinches give way to pockets and sidepulls past twelve bolts to anchors. (90')

H. Sun Dog 5.11a**
T. Caldwell
Letterbox pockets to reachy bulge. Eight bolts. (60')

I. Project

J. Very Zen 5.12c*
FA unknown
Rising rightwards through pinches, sidepulls, and tufas. Pass mid-station then left up streaked wall to chains. Twelve bolts. (95')

K. Sunburst 5.12c**
B. Ohran
Shares start with L, then left up wonderful tufa pinches to J's anchors. Eleven bolts. (100')

L. Boyle's Route 5.13a**
J. Pederson
Long and sustained route starting on slab and offering every feature possible through final bulge to chains. Eighteen bolts. (125')

THE BLACK WALL

A. Chuck Jones 5.11b*
B. Speed
Through blocky roof then edges and pockets to chains. Four bolts. (50')

B. Jack Purcell 5.11b*
B. Boyle
Pull roof on jugs then steep edges and pockets past four bolts to chains. (50')

C. Project

THE BURKE / BATEMAN WALL

A. Industrial Birdnesting 5.12a**
G. Burke
Named for a birds nest made out of bits of wire, plastic and foam. This route moves through blocky pinches to great pockets and huecos. Eight bolts to chains. (80')

B. Wild Eyed and Bushy Tailed 5.12a**
G. Burke
Small roof to cave-like huecos past ledge to pocket-laden scoop. Nine bolts to anchors. (95')

C. Blind Date 5.12b**
L. Bateman
Roof moves lead to smooth edge and pocket-filled wall. Eight bolts to chains. (80')

D. Even Flow 5.12c**
L. Bateman
Substantial roof to edges then big huecos. Ten bolts. (90')

SHOTHOLE CAVE

A. N/A 5.8
G. Burke, L. Bateman
Slab approach pitch past four bolts and runout to anchors. (60')

B. Shadow Line 5.11d***
L. Bateman, G. Burke
To right of small cave climb through huecos, overhangs and pockets to chains. Nine bolts. (120')

C. Project

D. Why Go Home 5.12b**
G. Burke
Dihedral moving right through bulge then great pockets and edges to anchors. Twelve bolts. (130')

THE FOSSIL CAVE

Access

Park on the southbound side of I-15 as for other climbing areas. Locate the approach trail to Virgin River and work north (upstream) to a crossing beneath the highway bridge (about 200 yards north of the parking area). Cross the river. This can be anywhere from knee deep to class 3 whitewater depending on conditions. Follow the ledge system north (upstream) working progressively higher above the river. A 15 minute hike along benches brings you to an obvious bandshell-like cave.

Note: Normal river crossing for this area is just downstream of the Shothole Cave Area. However, during periods of snowmelt or runoff the stream crossing may be very hazardous. The cable crossing and hike behind the hill entails unprotected 5th class climbing. Getting to this area may therefore prove to be hazardous, or at least arduous.

A. Ed's Labor 5.11b

E. Worseman

To the untrained eye this may appear to be a choss pile, but rumor has it that there is good climbing if you can stay on route. Ten bolts to chains. (85')

B. Homo Erectus 5.13a*

R. Leavitt

From top of block pinches, pockets, and edges through seven bolts. (85')

C. Cro Magnon 5.12c*

R. Leavitt

To right of small cave, this bouldery climb passes six bolts on pockets and jugs to chains. (50')

D. Primitive Man 5.13b**

R. Leavitt

Same start as C then depart right at fourth bolt through roof to chains. Eight bolts. (60')

E. Dynosaur 5.13c**

R. Leavitt

Same as D then traverse to steep roof with a dyno finish. Eleven bolts to chains. (90')

F. Project

G. Homo Sapien 5.13d***

R. Leavitt

Sustained steep pulling on slopers and edges all the way to the chains. Described as one of the best of its grade in the US.

DUTCHMAN'S
DRAW

Todd Perkins on Wind Brown Groan (5.12d)   Jorge Visser photo

DUTCHMAN DRAW - THE PHALANX OF WILL

The Arizona Strip, isolated from the remainder of the state by the Grand Canyon, is a region of few paved roads and remains one of the most remote areas in the lower 48. Driving on the rough dirt and gravel roads southeast of St. George one may believe this to be a vast wasteland of multicolored clay hills, crumbling lava flows, and barren plains that stretch, unbroken, towards the great chasm to the south. This would be a very mistaken premise, for lurking beneath the edge of appearances is a truly staggering amount of limestone gems (such as The Phalanx of Will) waiting to be discovered.

Lured to this seemingly profitless location by the promise of new crags, Glen Burke literally stumbled upon this immense tilted cube of stone while running up the wash one evening. Returning with local route developer Todd Perkins, the pair found a crack climb on the low angle back of the monolith offering 5.6 climbing to the top. Perkins and local Jorge Visser then spent several feverish months in a haze of dust and effort, drilling the hundreds of bolts that protect the long and sustained routes.

Contributions by Chad Perkins, Lea Hopkinson, and others helped make this remote and obscure location a worthwhile destination.

Season
The best conditions are between September and May. Elevation is 3500'.

Access
From St. George Blvd. drive east over the Interstate to River Road and turn right. Travel south for about 2.0 miles, cross the Virgin River and turn immediately left onto 1450 South. Hit your trip meter, all distances will be measured from here. The road curves left after 2.0 miles, crosses 3430 S, and curves right at 3.5 miles, just past the horse stables. At the 5.6 mile mark the road turns to graded gravel, bear left at the 8.5 mile mark and turn right at the 9.5 mile mark just past a pond and cattle loading chute. Road turns to dirt; bear left at the 10.5 mark; you are on BLM road 1035. Pass a pile of gypsum at 11.3 miles, and go under the powerlines at 13.2 miles. Continue straight through the four-way intersection passing a rusted truck at 13.8 miles, bear left at 14.0 miles and drive into the wash at 14.4 miles. 2WD vehicles park here and walk. 4WD's turn left up the wash and at 15.5 miles turn into the wash coming in from the left. Continue up this wash for 0.5 mile, and The Phalanx of Will is the obvious freestanding tower on the left.

Note: Climbers traveling in this area must be prepared! This region is remote, there are no facilities, and help would be a long way off in the event of breakdown or injury. Do not even attempt this approach in a passenger car. At a minimum, you'll want 2WD high clearance at a minimum and a 4WD to get in all the way.

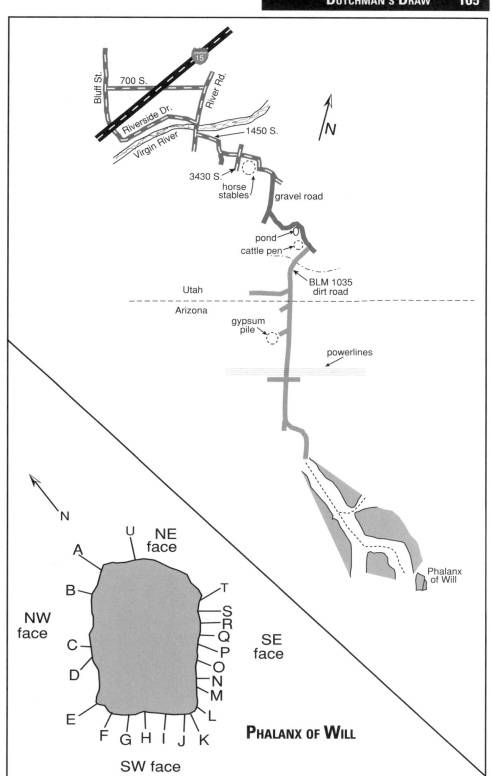

Phalanx of Will

Phalanx of Will

A. Ingrown Thumb Crack 5.6

T. Perkins, G. Burke

On the back side of the tower, an offwidth layback on low-angle rock leads to the summit. Medium to large pro. (100')

B. Coral Pores 5.11c**

T. Perkins, J. Visser

1st pitch: Sharp crimping on brown acmes. Eight bolts to chains. (5.10a)

2nd pitch: Steeper climbing past five bolts on crimpy blocks of brown rock. Five bolts to chains. (5.11c, 150')

C. A Nickel Bag of Funk 5.11c***

J. Visser, T. Perkins

Unique climbing on coral globules to horizontal break, then thin edges and crimpy pockets to chains. Eleven bolts. (150')

D. Open Project

E. Open Project

F. Broncos Baby 5.13a***

T. Perkins, J. Visser

Left of the prominent root, up slots and pinches in a shallow dihedral to bulge and chimney. Eighteen bolts. (160')

G. Fossil Eyes 5.14a***

T. Perkins, L. Hopkinson

Pinches and crimps up overhanging center of the southwest side. Fourteen bolts to chains. (110')

H. Va'ginia 5.12c**

J. Visser, T. Perkins

Dyno to crack at first bolt then sustained finger and hand jams to chains. Small to medium stoppers for supplemental gear. (50') Bolted face above anchor is a project.

I. Project

Departs to the left from anchors on H to anchors on G.

J. A Fossil of Mouse 5.13a/b***

T. Perkins, L. Hopkinson
Shares the first six bolts with K then left up face of flakes and edges in prominent dihedral to minor arete. Fifteen bolts. (110')

K. A Fossil of Man 5.13c/d***

T. Perkins, C. Perkins
Common start right onto overhanging arete on sustained crimpy sidepulls. Bulge to easier climbing and chains. Eighteen bolts. (130')

L. Open Project

M. The Pompetus Vision 5.12d***

T. Perkins, L. Hopkinson
Only Steve Miller knows what this is. Blocky pinches through scoop then up blunt prow on flakes and crimps to chains. Eleven bolts. (120')

N. Project

O. Frozen Snake Dance 5.13b***

T. Perkins, J. Visser
Crimp up edgy face past mid-station chains through horizontal break on blocky pinches and crimpy sidepulls to chains. Fourteen bolts. (120')

P. Windblown Groan 5.12d**

T. Perkins, C. Perkins
Sidepull flakes and acme crimps through bulge, then up concave face through second bulge to chains. Twelve bolts. (95')

Q. Cumulus Locos 5.12c*

T. Perkins, C. Perkins
Shares first three bolts with R, then left through bulge crossing left-leaning seam to O's chains below ledge. Eleven bolts. (90')

Katie Brown on Fossil of Man (5.13c/d)
Jorge Visser photo

R. Crystal Balls 5.12a**

T. Perkins, J. Visser

Common start leads to pockets with sloping gastons and underclings. Move right to flake, up seam and over bulge to chains. Fourteen bolts. (100')

S. Humboldt Haze 5.12c***

T. Perkins, L. Hopkinson

Prominent crack turning to seam with acmes on edges. Pull small roof at horizontal break, pass mid-station, and crimp acmes to chains. Ten bolts. (85')

T. One Bulge Wonder 5.12b*

T. Perkins, L. Hopkinson

Right of seam, follow flakes to small roof and acmes to R's chains. Ten bolts. (130')

U. Project

A new project on the N.E. face.

VARIATIONS:

Several link-ups have been done on the southeast face. Listed are the ones completed to date. The listing begins with the name of the route on which to begin, and subsequent names indicate the route to link into. Numbers in brackets indicated the bolt count at which to jump routes. Another method to sort this out is to ask a local.

N. FROZEN SNAKE DANCE

1. Frozen Groan 5.13b (5)
2. Frozen Groan Locos 5.13b (5),(5)
3. Frozen Groan Locos Balls 5.13b (5),(5),(5)

O. WINDBLOWN GROAN

1. Windblown Snake Dance 5.12d (2)
2. Windblown Locos 5.12c (7)
3. Windblown Locos Balls 5.12c (7),(5)

P. CUMULUS LOCOS

1. Cumulus Groan 5.12d (4)
2. Cumulus Balls 5.12a/b (9)

Q. CRYSTAL BALLS

1. Crystal Locos 5.12a (7)
2. Crystal Haze 5.12c (9)
   To midway anchors = Crystal 5.11c

R. HUMBOLDT HAZE

1. Humboldt Balls 5.11d (6)
   To midway anchors = Humboldt 5.11b
2. Humboldt Balls Locos 5.12a (6) (1)

S. ONE BULGE WONDER

1. One Bulge Haze 5.13a (6)

WEST CEDAR CRAGS

Bo Beck on Lick the Moss (5.11a)

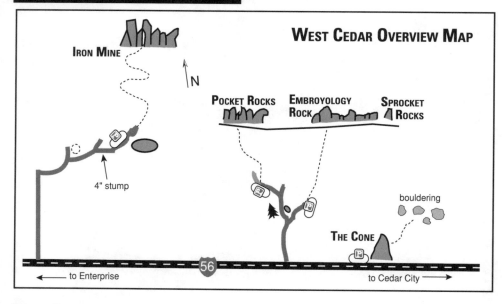

WEST CEDAR OVERVIEW MAP

IRON MINE

N

POCKET ROCKS   EMBROYOLOGY ROCK   SPROCKET ROCKS

4" stump

bouldering

THE CONE

to Enterprise   56   to Cedar City

THE CONE

Twelve miles west of Cedar City, and with a thirty second approach, The Cone offers three easy to moderate bolted routes on coarse welded tuff. Developed in 1995 by Iron County pioneer Bob Draney, this formation is the traditional venue where many of the locals get their first taste of the sport.

Recently, several motivated Cedar City climbers have been mining the bouldering potential in the area around The Cone, and have unearthed some excellent problems.

Season

This formation is at 6000' and faces south. Summer afternoons may be the only time it is unpleasant to climb here.

Access

From I-15 get off at the 1st Cedar Exit onto Main St. Follow Main St. North to Highway 56 (left at Lins Supermarket). Take Highway 56 west out of Cedar City for 12.0 miles. There is a large brown BLM "Public Lands" sign on the right, the formation is a couple hundred yards farther and is obvious on the right side of the road.

A. Electric Company 5.10a*

B. Draney, G. Wheeler

Facing west, the route follows pockets and nice edges through a bulge, past three bolts to the common anchor on the top. (30')

B. Power Conspiracy 5.9**

G. Wheeler, B. Draney

Friction on coarse welded tuff past four bolts to common anchor. (30')

C. Electric Avenue 5.7*

B. Draney, G. Wheeler

Resist the temptation to reach out and catch the electric wire at the top of this excellent beginner lead. Four bolts to common anchor. (30')

POCKET ROCKS

The first major sport climbing area developed west of Cedar City, the Pocket Rocks is a result of the pioneering efforts of Bob Draney, who in 1995 discovered the potential of the Sweet Hills just to the west of town.

Bob, his wife Katie, and several motivated friends

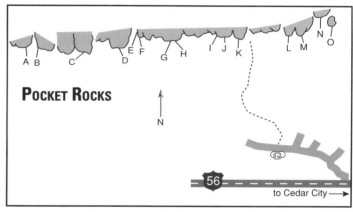

created a complete trail system, as well as a full spectrum of routes with grades from 5.9 to 5.11b.

The rock is a coarse welded tuff, crystalline in nature and similar in texture to quartz monzonite, yet much softer and less consolidated. The features that give the area its name result from impurities and softer materials getting trapped in the ash and eroding at a faster rate than the other rock. These pockets vary from sinker to sloper, and often have crystals around the edges that may break away and crumble. Suspect features aside, this area is well bolted, and offers enjoyable climbing in an aesthetic setting with excellent views of the sage and juniper hillsides.

Season

With a southern aspect, Pocket Rocks is most climbable in the spring and fall, though early morning in the summer is ideal. Winter brings snow that makes the access road impassable though the rock is still in a very climbable condition.

Access

From the stoplight on Main Street in Cedar City, drive west on Highway 56 for 12.2 miles. At the public lands sign, hit your trip meter and go 0.5 mile. Turn right onto a dirt road that weaves through the trees for 0.7 mile. Keep left at every intersection. You will know if this is the correct road if you need to squeeze between a rock and a tree. Park at the end of the road, and then back track on foot for 100' to the trail, which will take you west to the climbing area (15 minutes). If you don't find this area on your first attempt don't despair – it took me three tries.

POCKET ROCKS

A. Flake and Bake 5.11b**

C. Lloyd, N. Moorty

Steep face on pockets and edges through overlap to chains. Five bolts. (50')

B. Master Blaster 5.10d**

B. Draney, S. Luqe

Edges on beautiful brown patina to left of a big bird nest. Five bolts to chains. (50')

C. Shorty's Nightmare 5.10d

D. Mullens

Anyone's nightmare if you fall before the second bolt. Three bolts to chains on block under tree. (40')

D. Crunch Boy 5.10a*

B. Draney, K. Draney

Left trending route past five bolts on small block. Lap links on bolt hangers for anchors. (30')

E. Carnivorous Bitch 5.9*

B. Draney, G. Wheeler

A reference to Bob's dog, Mona, – though others may qualify. Four bolts on pocketed slab to chains. (50')

F. Mini - Houser Buttress 5.10a**

B. Draney, G .Wheeler

On a slender spire-like formation, five bolts on nice edges and pockets to shared chain anchor. (50')

G. Pocket Route 5.10b***

B. Draney, S. Luqe

There's a rumor of pockets on this. Five bolts to chains. (50')

H. Renacuajo (The Tadpole) 5.11a**

S. Luqe, B. Draney

Nice route on steep rock, pockets and crimps. Six bolts to common anchor. (50')

I. Chip's Crack 5.9

Chip somebody

Ten feet left of J, climb the splitter crack past some bushes. Belay from tree. Small to medium pro. (50')

J. Al Takes a Ride 5.10b**

B. Draney, G. Wheeler

Hopefully not with strangers. Pockets and edges on patina. Four bolts to chains. (40')

K. Utah Claw 5.10b**

B. Draney, G. Wheeler

Feminine hairstyle forming a claw-like feature in the front. Can be used as a skyhook if enough hairspray is used. Six bolts past edges and pockets to chains. (50')

L. It's Electrifying 5.9**

B. Draney, K. Draney

On spire-like buttress left of a bird nest, edge past four bolts. Clip chains from big rounded ledge. (50')

M. More Bolt's 5.10a*

T. Anderson

Long way to the first bolt on this edge and pocket route to the right of the bird nest. Four bolts to chains on rounded ledge. (50')

N. Sabie's Eight 5.9**

S. Luqe, B. Draney

Three bolts past pockets to chains. A nice route to warm up on. (40')

O. 5.10b TR

FA unknown

Steep start to good edges on this fun TR. Two-bolt anchor. (30')

P. Surmounting The Sumo 5.11*

T. Anderson

Thirty feet right of O, four bolts through pockets to a beautiful overhung bellyflop crux. Chain anchor. Not pictured. (40')

SPROCKET ROCKS

Beginning with the Embryology Crack formation, Iron County locals Troy Anderson, Pete VanSlooten and Nate Williams began to develop the block-like formations along the ridge line above the Cone in 1997. Though not exceedingly high, the variety and number of routes certainly justify the steep hike up the hillside to this pleasant and remote area.

Sprocket Rocks differs from the other formations in this area by the scarcity of pockets on many of the routes. A hard outer patina has formed a pleasant variety of edges on these small blocks. These routes require a combination of technical footwork and calloused fingertips to withstand the coarse and abrasive nature of the crystal-like edges.

Season

As with Pocket Rocks, this area is at 6000' with a southern exposure, and thus spring and fall offer optimum conditions. Summer mornings are also a good bet as would be sunny winter afternoons, except the road and trail may be snow covered.

Access

Drive west on Highway 56 for 12.2 miles from main street in Cedar City. One-half mile past the BLM "Public Lands" sign, turn right onto a unmarked dirt road. When passing under the power lines make a right turn, drive down a steep hill, and then back up the other side. Park and locate a trail marked with cairns, and follow this up the hill to the climbing area. Alternately, the Embryology Rock is prominent on the ridge — simply head uphill toward this formation.

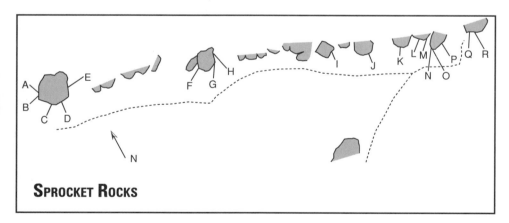

SPROCKET ROCKS

Embryology Rock

A. Fiesta At Elmo's 5.7**

P. VanSlooten, N. Williams
Variation to B. Slab past three
bolts to chains. (35')

B. Super Groover 5.8**

P. VanSlooten, N. WIlliams
Three bolts and medium pro
placement to chains on slab.
(35')

C. Embryology Crack 5.10**

B. Draney, S. Luqe
Prominent right-leaning crack.
Small to medium pro. Chain
anchor. (35')

D. League Night 5.11

T. Anderson
Thin right-arching crack to
face. Four bolts and small gear
to chains. (35')

E. Project

Sprocket Rocks

F. Erie Heights 5.10d*

P. VanSlooten, N. Williams
Four bolts up flake in shallow dihedral. Chain anchor. Not pictured.
(35')

G. Project

H. Project

I. Rimjob 5.12b/c*

R. Culbert
Hard crimping to slab. Three bolts to
chains. (30')

J. Get Fixed 5.11**

T. Anderson
Four bolts on this fun and edgy face.
Chain anchor. (35')

K. De-Appendix Day 5.11b**

P. VanSlooten

Nice pockets and crimps past four bolts to sling anchor. (35')

L. Ticks on Parade 5.10**

S. Durfee, T. Anderson

Stem behind block to reach crack to left of roof. Medium to large pro. Shares anchor with M. (45')

M. Missy's Playhouse 5.8***

T. Anderson

Bolted chimney, then stem onto face. Four bolts to chains. (40')

N. Septic Death 5.6

T. Stephens, T. Anderson

Three bolts on slab with large holds. Shares anchor with O. (30')

O. Line Between Light and Dark 5.10d***

N. Williams

Three bolts on steep arete to chains. (30')

P. White Harlem 5.11d**

R. Culbert

Steep crimping past three bolts to chains. (30')

Q. Lip Before Clip 5.10**

T. Anderson

Technical edging on steep slab. Five bolts to sling anchor. (35')

R. Cedar Variation 5.10*

T. Anderson

Three bolt variation up edges to last bolt of Q. (35')

THE IRON MINE

Iron County is so named for the iron prevalent in the Sweet Hills to the west of Cedar City. A large open pit mine with associated tailings dominates the landscape just across the valley from this remote and nicely developed climbing area. The Iron Mine area was developed by the ubiquitous Bob Draney and his posse of friends in 1995.

Similar to Pocket Rocks in both rock type and climbing features, The Iron Mine offers both longer routes than Pockets as well as a few traditional lines for variety. At the parking area, the Iron Mine boulder also offers the opportunity to sample some of the best boulder problems in the region. The twenty foot high boulder has over fifteen problems and topropes mostly in the 5.10 to 5.12 range. There are bolts on the top for anchors.

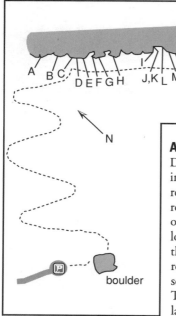

IRON MINE

Season

The Iron Mine area is climbable from mid-spring to late fall with summer mornings being ideal. The wall is at 6000' and faces west.

Access

Drive west on Highway 56 for 16.3 miles from Main St. intersection in Cedar City. Turn right onto a well graded dirt road at mile marker 44. Drive 2.8 miles and turn right at a road that says: "Private road do not enter" Go 1.1 miles, over a hill and turn right just before a corral. Go 0.4 mile looking for another dirt road on the right that heads towards the cliff. Take this road, passing over a 4" stump in the road, and park by the boulder. There is a trail on the southeast corner of the boulder that switchbacks to the crag. These dirt roads may be impassable in the early spring and late fall due to snow and mud.

Note: you will be passing over private property to access this crag. Follow these directions and drive slowly to avoid conflicts with the landowners.

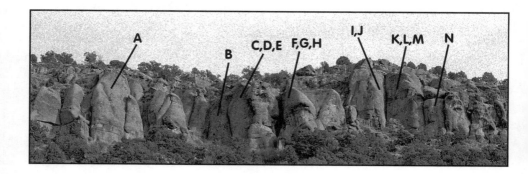

The Iron Mine

A. Sebastian's Pillar Crack 5.10a*

S. Luqe, B. Draney

Crack between wall and pillar to face moves left to another crack. Hands to crux overhang and slab to top. Medium to large pro. (120') Walk off.

B. No Sweat 5.9+*

B. Draney

Slightly overhanging face climb protected with medium to large gear in pockets. (65')

C. Standard Deviation 5.10b*

B. Draney, G. Wheeler

Vertical face climbing on hollow flakes and pockets past ten bolts to rap anchor. (70')

D. Confidence Interval 5.10c**

B. Draney, G. Wheeler

Up the middle of the block on pockets and flakes past ten bolts to common anchor. (70')

E. Project

F. Project

G. Inspired by Gravity 5.12a*

B. Draney, G. Wheeler

Slopey pockets through overhang to chains. Nine bolts. (75')

H. Project

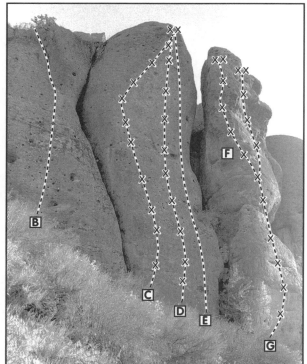

I. Just Defy 5.11a/b**

B. Draney, G. Wheeler

Patina covered faceholds lead to height dependent deadpoint and edges to anchors. Five bolts. (55')

J. Go For Nad's 5.12a*

B. Draney, G. Wheeler

Contrived route avoiding the good holds to the right. Crimp through five bolts to common anchor. (55')

K. Vesicular Manslaughter 5.10b**

B. Draney, G. Wheeler

The natural line clipping five bolts to the left. (55')

L. Holy Buckets 5.10a**

B. Draney

Big pockets up beautiful vertical wall. Six bolts to chains. (50')

M. Lick the Moss 5.11a***
S. Luqe, B. Draney
Nice sustained route with committing move at top. Eight bolts to chain anchor. (55')

N. A Fine Mine Line 5.11b/c*
B. Draney
Platform to steep pocketed face. Four bolts to chains. (40')

Access:
The Iron Eagle Buttress is located 200 yards to the south, along the same ridge line.

Note: a small cavern just before the formation is a snake den, where rattlesnakes are prevalent.

O. Iron Lung 5.12b**
T. Goss, B. Beck

P. Iron Eagle 5.12a**
T. Goss, I. Horn
Crimp up patina face to ledge and pockets to rap anchor. Eight bolts. (65')

CEDAR CANYON CRAGS

Steve Platt climbing on the Cetacean Wall

THE CETACEAN WALL

The first wall in Cedar Canyon developed as a sport crag, the Cetacean Wall offers numerous climbs in the 5.11 to 5.12 grades, nice views of the canyon, and a minimal approach.

The rock is a soft limestone which feels similar to sandstone, and forms comparable edges, pockets, and sloping shelves which often require bold and awkward mantles. The crag was developed primarily by Bob Draney who spent many weekends between attending classes at SUU bolting and cleaning lines.

Season
The Cetacean Wall is climbable from late spring through the fall. The wall gets morning sun, but is deep in the shade by the afternoon — making it a good bet on a hot summer day.

Access
From St. George take I-15 north to Cedar City. Take the first exit which becomes Main Street. Continue north to an intersection with Center Street (Highway 14) and turn right. Drive 9.3 miles up Cedar Canyon on Highway 14, and park at a pullout on the left. Cross the road and locate a trail about 100' up from the parking area. Cross the stream just above a beautiful pool and follow the trail to the wall (two minutes).

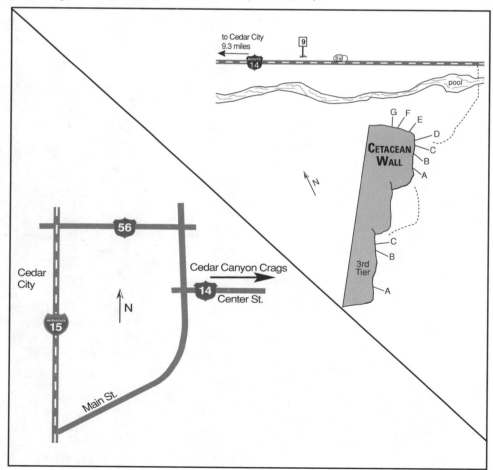

CETACEAN WALL—FIRST TIER

A. Fragment "G" 5.12a*

B. Draney, S. Luqe

To the left of the chossy roof, follow five bolts past crimps, pebbles, and blocks to chains. (50')

B. Booga Beluga 5.11a/b**

B. Draney, S. Luqe

Right of the choss roof, a crack leads to nice edges and crimps past four bolts to chains. Medium pro is helpful. (50')

C. Sound Image 5.11c

B. Draney, S. Luqe

Left tending route past five bolts to chains near big block. (50')

D. Tursiops Leap 5.12b/c**

S. Luqe, B. Draney

On corner beneath big block climb edges and mantles past six bolts to chains on block. (50')

E. Wailing 5.12a/b*

B. Draney, S. Luqe

Right of spruce tree, six bolts lead past edges to chains. (50')

F. Sailing 5.11d**

S. Luqe, B. Draney

Before corner, climb past five bolts and serious crimps to chains. (50')

G. Bailing 5.12a**

B. Draney, S. Luqe

Around corner, five bolts through crimps and height dependent dead-point. Shares anchor with route F. (50')

3RD TIER

A. Spaceboy 5.10b TR
FA unknown
Nice variety of holds on this fun toprope. Two-bolt anchor set up from the left. (45')

B. Fluffhead 5.11c*
B. Draney
To left of roof climb through six bolts worth of edges and pockets. (45')

C. Limeboy 5.12a*
FA unknown
To right of the roof. Somewhat height dependent. Six bolts. (45')

Steve Platt on Tursiops Leap (5.12b/c)

GRAVESIDE MATTER WALL

When new route activist Bob Draney departed in 1996, a gaping void was left in the Iron County climbing community. With many undeveloped areas surrounding them, Troy Anderson, Tyler Phillips, Pete VanSlotten and Nate Brown assumed the mantle of local route developers. They didn't have to look far to discover the wealth of possibilities that Cedar Canyon had to offer. The Graveside Matter Wall is basically across the street from the Cetacean Wall. Named for the memorial cross that commemorates the site of a rappeling death in 1996, the wall offers steep slab climbing as well as vertical and overhanging affairs. This area compliments the Cetacean Wall nicely with more moderate grades and different styles of climbing.

Season

The Graveside Matter Wall is climbable from early spring to late fall depending on the snow conditions. The wall gets morning shade and late afternoon sun, the opposite of the Cetacean Wall which will extend many climbing days.

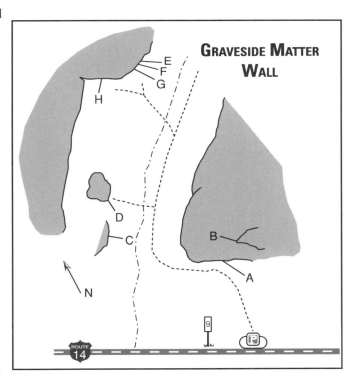

Access

From Main St. in Cedar City turn on Center St. (Hwy 14). Drive 9.3 miles up Cedar Canyon Road (also Route 14), and park at the pullout on the left. This is essentially beneath the Adventure Climb Arete. Follow the trail past Not Free Yet and around the corner to the right, passing Gotta Have Nuts traverse across the wash on the left. Continue up the trail 100 yards looking for a left-side trail. Cross the wash to the wall on the left.

"The aim of life is to live, and to live means to be aware, joyously, drunkenly, serenely, divinely aware."
- Henry Miller

GRAVESIDE MATTER AREA

A. Not Free Yet 5.10 A0*

T. Anderson

Two bolts (A0) lead to hand and finger crack. TCU's to #3 Camalot for pro. (65')
Belay off large tree at the top.

B. The Adventure Climb 5.10***

P. VanSlooten, T. Phillips

On the slab arete above route A. Nice exposure and views of the canyon on this esthetic
route. Eight bolts to two-bolt anchor. (70')

C. Gotta Have Nuts 5.10c*

P. VanSlooten

Up trail around corner from route A, just on the other side of the creek bed. Traverse
either left or right —weird but cool— using slots and cracks for pro. Small to medium
pro. Must be followed by a second to clean.

D. Fallout 5.11c***

N. Brown, T. Phillips

Fifty yards up trail, take a side trail to a buttress sitting above the wash. The route is on
the arete towards the canyon and follows four bolts through a crimpy crux to a two-bolt
anchor. (50')

GRAVESIDE MATTER WALL

E. Widowmaker 5.10d* R/X

P. VanSlooten
Just to left of the tree.
Friction up slab using small
cracks for sketchy pro to
common anchor. TCU's to
#4 Camalot. (50')

F. Faceplant 5.10a***

T. Phillips, P. VanSlooten
Friction slab through
overlaps, five bolts to
common anchor. (50')

G. Ghost Rider 5.6**

P. VanSlooten, T. Phillips
Low-angle friction past four
bolts arching right to a
common anchor. (50')

H. Too Much Chalk, Not Enough Lycra 5.12a***

P. VanSlooten
Thirty yards to left of F up steep wall past
six bolts to height dependent crux. Two-
bolt anchor. Name pokes fun at a
previous guidebook's name. (65')

THE 10 MILE WALL

Just over a 0.5 mile further up the canyon from the Cetacean Wall parking area, the 10 Mile Wall offers yet another style of climbing in this small but diverse area. The routes, steep slabs bolted on lead, are a rarity in an age of overhanging walls bolted on rappel. Most local routes of this nature are things done years ago with old bolts of suspect integrity, but this wall offers recent routes with reliable bolts done in a style which one only begins to respect when on the route.

Season

This wall is at just over 6000' and faces northeast, resulting in morning sun and afternoon shade throughout most of the year. Winter is the only unclimbable season on this wall.

Access

Drive 10.0 miles up Cedar Canyon and park on the right just after the 10 mile marker. The wall is obvious on the right, and requires a five minute hike to get to.

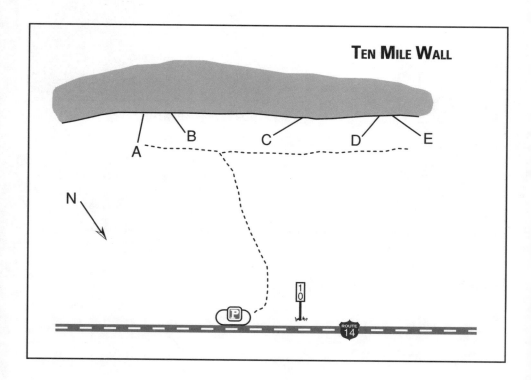

A. Project

B. Staying Alive 5.10

T. Phillips, N. Brown

Friction slab past two bolts to flake, then two more bolts to a tree for anchor at the top of the slab. Small to medium pro. (60')

C. Psycho Slab Addict 5.10c*

T. Anderson, P. VanSlooten

Right of tree, follow five bolts up the slab to a two-bolt anchor. (60')

D. Saturday Night Fever 5.11b*

T. Phillips, T. Anderson

Serious friction on this slab test piece. Five bolts to tree belay. (60')

E. I Hate The World 5.10d*

T. Anderson, L. Harvey

On right side of the wall, friction past five bolts to common tree anchor. (60')

PAROWAN

Mike Tupper on Last of the Mohechans (5.12d)

SHINOBE

The popularity and quality of the cobble climbing at Maple Canyon has caused climbers to look at conglomerate cliffs in a new light. Long dismissed as to chossy or lacking natural lines, cobblestone cliffs are now being developed in many areas of the country as climbers discover the unique style of climbing this surface provides.

Bob Draney bolted the first five routes here in 1994, selecting a short clean wall of bullet proof cobbles 20 minutes up a canyon to the west of the main formation. Bob called the area Parowon Gap in reference to the area's proximity (2.0 miles) to the nationally renowned petroglyph site further up the gravel road.

In September 1996, intent on climbing Bob's routes, Todd Goss and Ian Horn took a look at the main formation, and were dumbfounded at the sheer quantity of climbing to be had here. Returning the next day laden with enough bolts and battery power to start an ethical war, the pair began the route development in earnest.

Feeling that people may think that they were climbing on or near the petroglyphs, they named the main formation Shinobe, after the Anasazi trickster god who disguises himself as a coyote.

Season

Shinobe is at 6000' and faces south which makes it climbable year round. Summer mornings find the wall in the shade till noon, and afternoons in the winter are often excellent. Because of the natural wind funnel effect of the Parowon Gap, the crag can often be very windy – a plus on a hot day, but miserable in the cold.

Access

From Interstate 15 take either Parowon exit and turn onto Gap Road from Main Street (follow the signs that say "Petroglyphs"). Stay on this road for 11.0 miles, past the dry lake bed, through some low hills, and the formation will be obvious on the right. Park in the field on the left, and follow the trail to the right side of the formation.

Note: There are several raptor species that nest on this cliff. Please give them the space they need. It would be good to avoid climbing here, especially if there are nesting birds present, from March to July.

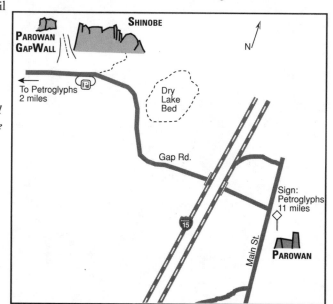

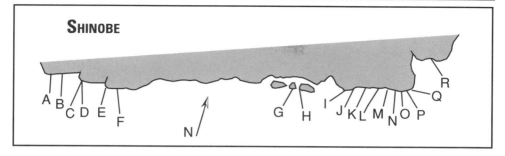

SHINOBE

SHINOBE

A. Project

B. Project

C. Chains of Freedom 5.12a*

> *T. Goss, D. Biniaz*
> Cobble slab to pockets in bulge. Fifteen bolts to rap anchor. (170')
> *Note: route requires 60 meter rope!*

D. Chains of Passion 5.10b**

> *T. Goss, E. Jones*
> A nice way off without the hard part of route C. Ten bolts to rap anchor. (100')

E. Vast Deserts of Contemplation 5.11b**

> *T. Goss, E. Jones*
> Great pockets to tricky bulge. Six bolts to rap anchors. (65')
> *Note: The first bolt hanger has been hammered flat so bring a stick clip.*

F. Set in Stone 5.11c**

> *D. Biniaz, T. Goss*
> Hard start leads to nice pockets. Five bolts to rap anchor. Not pictured. (60')

G. A Dangerous but Irresistible Pastime 5.12a**

T. Goss, I. Horn

Steep pumpy arete on nice pockets. Four bolts to rap anchor. (40')

H. Project

I. Desperately Seeking Oxygen 5.12c***

T. Goss, I. Horn

Overhanging pockets in a water streak, leads to a football cobble and easier climbing above. Seven bolts to rap anchor. (70')

J. The Last of the Mohicans 5.12d***

M. Tupper, E. Tupper

Steep cobbles (one looks like Perot's ear) to more of the same. Eight bolts to rap anchor. (75')

K. Dancing Katchinas 5.12b**

T. Goss, I. Horn

Cobble pulling past one ghastly big bastard, then up water channel on nice pockets. Eight bolts to rap anchor. (75')

L. The Winds of Change 5.11d**

I. Horn, T. Goss

Nice cobbles to blunt arete, and hard to find pockets. Seven bolts to rap anchor. (70')

M. Effigy 5.11a**

T. Goss, I. Horn

Reachy start leads to good pocket climb. Six bolts to rap anchor. (60')

N. Baked Potato 5.10a**

I. Horn, T. Goss

Pockets and cobbles in a vertical wall. Five bolts to rap anchor. (50')

O. Tin-Man 5.10b**

T. Goss, I. Horn

Just need a heart for this one. Five bolts to rap anchor. (50')

P. No More Mr. Nice Guy 5.10d*

T. Goss, I. Horn

A gift project "reclaimed". One hard move on nice pockets. Five bolts to rap anchors. (50')

Q. Screaming Banshee's 5.8*

A. Barnard, T. Goss

Hard to focus on your first FA with six screaming kids. Four bolts to common anchor. (45')

R. Coyote Waits 5.8**

E. Tupper, M. Tupper

Great pockets in nice rock. Seven bolts to rap anchor. (75')

PAROWON GAP

Access

Hike up gully to the west of the formation for 20 minutes. The Wall is on the left and faces southwest. Easily recognized by a large detached block on the left side.

A. Sheeka 5.7*

B. Draney
Crack in corner off to left of main wall. Small to medium pro. (40)'

B. Cobble Stoned 5.10c**

B. Draney
To the right of the detached block, climb pockets and cobbles past four bolts to anchor. (40')

C. Pray to the Feather 5.11c**

B. Draney
Cobbles in bomber matrix past six bolts to shared anchor with B. (45')

D. Soaring Overhead 5.12a**

B. Draney
Steep slopy cobble pulling. Five bolts to two-bolt anchor. (40')

E. Mouth Music 5.12a*

B. Draney
Through overhang past five bolts to anchor. Stick clip recommended. (40')

Darl Binaz enjoys A Dangerous but Irrestible Pastime (5.12a)

BRIAN HEAD

Michal Nad on Smiling at the Majorettes (5.11b)

THE OVERLOOK

At an elevation of almost 11,000 feet, The Overlook provides the best bet to beat the oppressive heat of southern Utah summers. Up here, amidst the spruce and aspen groves, the distant tap of a woodpecker or the cry of a circling raven often answers the whistling of marmots. With a spectacular view of the Parowon Valley and the smell of the conifers in the air, the fact that we can also climb here often seems to good to be true.

Rumor has it that Amy Whistler climbed many of the cracks here while working at the Brian Head Resort in the early 80's, but it wasn't until 1993 that Bob Draney began route development in earnest, putting up many of the early classics. Todd Goss and numerous friends did most of the remaining routes over the summers of '96 and '97.

The area consists of blocks of welded tuft which offer pocket climbing on clean, sometimes polished faces. This rock differs from other local tuft areas in that it is much less granular, and more compact.

The routes here range from vertical pockets and cracks to wild aretes and short steep faces. The harder climbs feature one and two-finger pockets seemingly made for pulling on.

Season
Definitely a summer only area. The opening day, dependent on the winter's snowpack, comes sometimes as late as mid-June. Fall brings cooler temperatures and fantastic colors. The aspen trees turn gold, and signal an end to climbing around mid-October as the first snow closes the road.

Access
From Main St. in Cedar City turn East on Center St. (Hwy 14) and drive through Cedar Canyon to Hwy 148 (18.0 miles). Turn left here and drive through Cedar Breaks National Monument to Hwy 143 (7.0 miles). Turn east onto highway 143 and travel towards Panguich Lake for 4.7 miles. Turn left onto the Sidney Valley dirt road and continue straight for another 4.4 miles to the turnaround at the overlook.

Note: Many routes have just two-bolt anchors at the top with regular hangers. You can retrieve your anchor draws from the top of the formations.

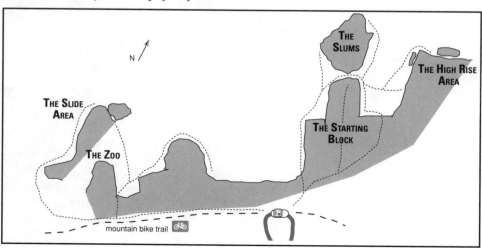

THE OVERLOOK- THE SLIDE AREA

A. Crime Doesn't Pay 5.11a*
T. Goss, P. Auerbach
Three bolts past pockets and awkward edges. Rap anchor. (30')

B. Stolen Thunder 5.10c*
T. Goss, P. Auerbach
FA during a thunderstorm. Three bolts to common anchor. (30')

C. Trads Make Me Laugh 5.10a**
T. Goss, R. Foster
Pocketed face to the right of a crack. Four bolts to a two-bolt anchor. (40')

D. Clippin' Cams Not Bolts 5.10b**
T. Phillips
Climbs the cracks to the left of C. Medium to large pro. (40')

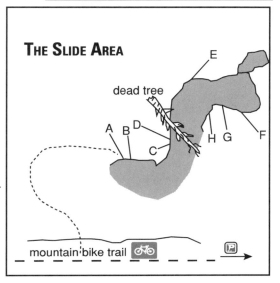

E. Lost Cause 5.11c*
T. Goss, D. Biniaz
Dihedral to face to arete. Eight bolts to rap anchor. (65')

F. AC/DC Crack 5.9*
T. Phillips
To the right of the window. Thirty foot long splitter. Medium to large pro. Gear anchor. Descent: traverse left to corner and rap.

G. Window Crack 5.10b*
P. VanSlooten, T. Phillips
Crack above window up to rap anchor. Medium pro. (30')

H. Reconcilliation 5.12b**
T. Goss, E. Jones
Steep pockets lead to vertical, lichen covered face. Four bolts to rap anchor. (40')

THE OVERLOOK- THE ZOO

A. Midget Marathon 5.10a*

T. Goss, J. Truelove
Three bolts up mossy pockets. Two-bolt anchor. (30')

B. It's No Secret 5.11b***

B. Draney, K. Draney
Four bolts on arete. Great pockets! Chain anchor. (35')

C. Orange Krush 5.12b**

T. Goss, M. Nad
Steep pockets, then pull roof via hard-to-see dyno. Five bolts. (40')

D. Dwarf Tossing 5.12b/c**

T. Goss, D. Biniaz
Hard start, beautiful stone. Three bolts to rap anchor. (30')

E. Oxygen Deficit 5.12b/c**

T. Goss, D. Biniaz
Steep pockets through roof. Five bolts to a two-bolt anchor. (40')

F. Fits of Rage 5.12d***

T. Goss, J. Truelove
Hard moves through bulge to sequential monos. Six bolts to a two-bolt anchor. (50')

G. Angst 5.12a**

T. Goss, R. Fisher
White streak with pockets. Six bolts to two-bolt anchor. (55')

H. How Ya' Lichen It 5.11a*

T. Goss, R. Fisher
Orange and green streaked lichen face littered with pockets. Four bolts to two-bolt anchor. (45')

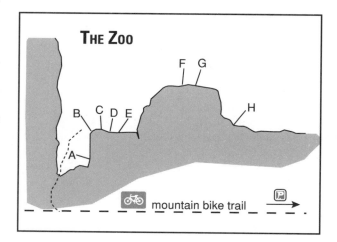

THE ZOO

mountain bike trail

Chris Cluff on Smiling at the Majorities (5.11b)

THE OVERLOOK- THE STARTING BLOCK

A. Willie the Pimp 5.10a***

T. Goss, J. Truelove

Blocky overhangs through roof on pockets to vertical face. Five bolts to sling anchor. (50')

B. Suck It Up Crybaby 5.12b***

T. Goss, J. Nad

Overhanging shelves to sharp arete via six bolts worth of hard pocket pulling. Two-bolt anchor. (50')

C. Must Suck Being You 5.12b/c**

T. Goss, R. Fisher

Steep, soft rock to lichen-streaked pocketed face. Six bolts to a two-bolt anchor. (50')

D. Pumping Out of Gas 5.11a*

T. Goss, R. Fisher

Awkward moves to attain ledge then pockets. Five bolts to a two-bolt anchor. (45')

E. Funky Boss 5.10c**

N. Moorty

Should've been called Funky Slopers! Pockets past five bolts to chains. (50')

F. No Rhyme or Reason 5.10a

B. Draney, K. Draney

Hard start can be avoided by heading right. Medium gear in crack then stem past two bolts to a two-bolt anchor. (50')

G. Blue Suede Shoes 5.12a***

B. Draney, K. Draney

Proceed through chossy scoop onto arete. Five bolts to lowering rings. (40')

H. Howard Hughes 5.11c***

B. Draney, K. Draney

Classic pockets in a smooth wall. Four bolts to two-bolt anchor. (40')

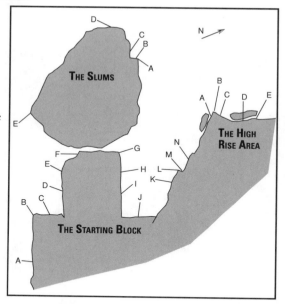

Rich Hurd on Blue Suede Shoes (5.12a)

I. Heimie the Mexican Gynecologist 5.11d**

T. Goss, A. Jones

Black streak with pockets. Four bolts to two-bolt anchor. Named after the original route developer in Chihuahua, Mexico. (30')

J. Dr. Diaper 5.9*

B. Draney, K. Draney

Thirty foot splitter crack. Small to medium pro to chain anchor. (35')

K. As The Song and Dance Begins 5.9*

T. Goss, D. Biniaz

Pockets in a slab past three bolts to two-bolt anchor. (30')

L. Dirty Rotten Scoundrel 5.10b*

B. Draney, K. Draney

Around the corner from K, climb crack up face then right to arete. Small to medium pro. Use gear for anchor. (40')

M. What's My Line 5.9

FA unknown

Two bolts in stemming corner to two-bolt anchor. (25')

N. Angering The Cheese Gods 5.10b**

T. Goss, D. Biniaz

Fun four bolt edge and pocket route to two-bolt anchor. (35')

THE OVERLOOK- THE HIGH RISE AREA

A. Orifice 5.8*
B. Draney, K. Draney

Offwidth crack between the main wall and a detached block. Large pro needed (duh!). Use tree on top for anchor. (40')

B. Virtual Ecstasy 5.11c***
T. Goss, R. Fisher

Awesome arete with pockets on both sides. Five bolts to a two-bolt anchor. (50')

C. The Crucible 5.12d/13a***
T. Goss, H. Christenson

Tiny monos and crimps on this technical route. Five bolts to a two-bolt anchor. (50')

D. Birth Canal 5.11d**
T. Goss, D. Biniaz

Scramble up gully behind block. Five bolts up pockets and edges. Two-bolt anchor. (50')

E. Project

F. One Finger Pockets Suck 5.10a**
N. Brown, T. Phillips

Splitter crack to sling anchors. Medium to large pro. (45')

THE OVERLOOK- THE SLUMS

A. Smiling At The Majorettes 5.11b***

B. Draney, K. Draney

Initial loose rock gives way to nice edges on inspiring arete. Six bolts to chains. (65')

B. Smoking Winston Cigarettes 5.11c*

B. Draney, K. Draney

Right of the arete, vertical edging and pockets. Six bolts to chains. (65')

C. Mercy Street 5.11d**

T. Goss, R. Fisher

To the right of corner, a chossy start gives way to edges on a beautiful face. Six bolts to rap anchor. (65')

D. Angle of Repose 5.12a***

T. Goss, R. Foster

Starting at a razor sharp block, climb through loose rock to incredibly featured face. Pull roof off of a mono-undercling. Eleven bolts to rap anchor. Stick clipping the first bolt is recommended. (83')

E. Slum Lords 5.11c*

T. Goss, A. Barnard

Around the corner and uphill 50 meters from D. Steep pocket pulling leads to committing move at third bolt. Six bolts to rap anchor. (50')

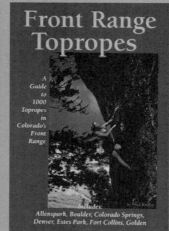

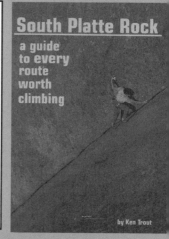
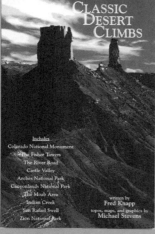

THE RUNNING SCARED WALL (AKA RAVENS CRAG)

With new route development reaching a feverish pace at The Overlook, little attention was given to this basalt crag that peeks above the aspen trees just north of the Sidney Valley Road. However, as The Overlook began to be climbed out, several first ascentionists looked towards this crag for possible development.

Tyler Phillips made the initial foray into the wall in May 1998 and soloed a 5.5 crack on the right side of the formation. While hiking out through the woods he noticed noises behind him that would stop when he stopped. Upon reaching the open meadow, he turned and looked towards the crag and saw a mountain lion watching him from the treeline. Tyler named both the route and crag Running Scared for the spooked out feeling he had in the woods.

In July of that same year Todd Goss and Darl Biniaz began bolting the Dark Tower. Goss also spent several weekends with Erin Jones developing the surrounding areas, with Jones constructing the luxury trail to the crag. Unaware of the Phillips story Goss named the crag for the congregation of ravens that soared over the Dark Tower every afternoon, acknowledging that the crag was theirs and climbers are only visitors.

Though only 35 to 60 feet in height, this area makes up for its diminutive height by offering a variety of grades as well as styles of climbing from cracks to dihedrals to faces to aretes.

Situated in an aspen glade, and offering astounding views from the top of the routes, this area is magical in the fall as the surrounding trees turn breath-taking colors.

Season
Depending on the winter snowpack at this 9000' crag, climbing is possible from May through October. The wall receives morning shade and afternoon sun.

Access
From Main St. in Cedar City turn East on Center St. (Hwy 14) and drive through Cedar Canyon to Hwy 148 (18.0 miles). Turn left (north) and drive through Cedar Breaks National Monument to Hwy 143 (7.0 miles). Turn right (east) for 5.5 miles toward Panguich Lake. The crag is visible above the trees on the left. Continue beyond the wall to a large pullout on the right. Cross the road and head uphill, through the woods to an old logging road. Turn left and find the trail to the crag, which is marked with blue ribbon and cairns. High clearance vehicles can continue on Rt. 143 for 2.0 miles to the start of this logging road on the left just past the county sign. Turn left onto a rough dirt road and drive west for 2.0 miles to trail marked with cairns on the right.

"Faith may be defined briefly as an illogical belief in the occurence of the improbable."
- H.L. Mencken

Lyle Hurd on a project at the Running Scared Wall

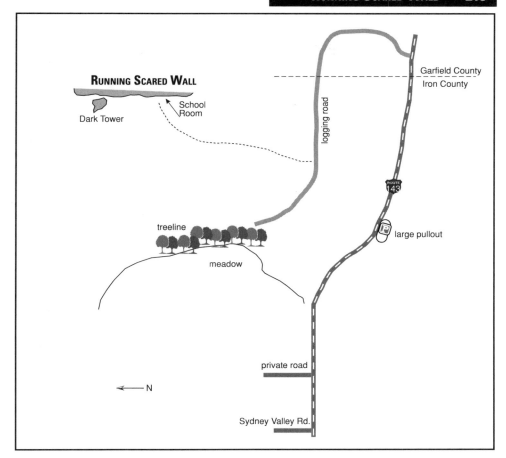

THE DARK TOWER AREA

A. Blackbird Fly 5.9**
T. Goss, E. Jones
Pockets and big edges on this four-bolt slab. Rap anchor. (35')

B. Project

C. Old Grandfather 5.11b***
T. Goss, L. Hurd
Balancy edges lead to great arete. Five bolts to rap anchor. (35')

D. Soaring Shadow 5.8+**
T. Goss, E. Jones
Low angle face right of arete. Four bolts to common anchor. (40')

E. Ravenous 5.9**
T. Goss, E. Jones
Ever steepening wall of edges. Four bolts to rap anchor. No photo due to trees. (35')

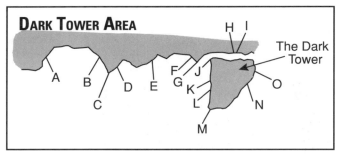

F. Stem It If You Get It 5.9*

T. Phillips, A. Seals

Shallow dihedral to the right of blunt arete. Small to medium pro. Use route G's anchor. (35')

G. Project

H. Black Soul 5.10b**

T. Goss, E. Jones

Chimney until it gets too wide, then pull on reachy pockets past four bolts to rap anchor. (45')

I. Orange Desperado 5.9+

T. Phillips, A. Seals

Splitter cracks through orange lichen and birdshit. Small to medium pro. Walk off to descend. (40')

J. Flights of Fancy 5.11d***

T. Goss, E. Jones

Short arete past three bolts and some hard pulls. Stick clip the first bolt! Rap anchor. (35')

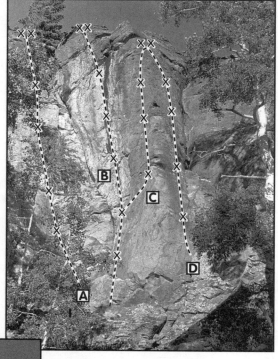

K. Feathered Friends 5.11a***

T. Goss, E. Jones

Shares start with L then balancy moves to the left. Killer pockets to the rap anchors. Ten bolts. (50')

L. Project

M. Raven Lunatic 5.12a***

T. Goss, D. Biniaz

From tree, through crimpy bulge to ledge then up right to arete, hard reachy crimps to pockets. Nine bolts to rap anchor. (60')

N. The Dog's Bollocks 5.10b**

T. Goss, E. Jones

Delicate climbing on flakes leads to nice edges and pockets. Seven bolts lead to anchors. (60')

O. Heart of Darkness 5.11a**

T. Goss, E. Jones

Powerful traverse leads to easier ground above. Seven bolts to rap anchor. (60')

Dark Tower Area

H,I, and J not pictured due to trees.

H. Conjunction 5.8**
T. Goss, E. Jones
Clean and edgy
face climbing past
four bolts to rap
anchors. (40')

I. Running Scared 5.5*
T. Phillips solo
Connect discon-
tinuous cracks on
this nice slab. Rap
anchor. (40')

J. Junction 5.7**
T. Goss, E. Jones
Big holds and
edges on this fun
four-bolt slab.
Rap anchor. (40')

THE SCHOOL ROOM AREA

A. Common Denominator 5.8**
T. Goss, E. Jones
Looks a lot worse than it is!
Four bolts through positive
holds. Rap anchor. (40')

B. Tastes Like Chicken 5.7+**
T. Phillips, A. Seals
Shallow corner to the right of A.
Medium to large pro. Walk off.
(40')

C. Continental Drift 5.10b**
T. Goss, E. Jones
Short overhang leads to nice
edges. Four bolts to rap anchor.
(40')

D. Categorical Imperative 5.9*
T. Goss, E. Jones
From top of ramp, four bolts
lead through edges and pockets.
Rap anchor. (40')

E. Hankering for Recess 5.8*
T. Goss, E. Jones
Slightly easier version of D.
Four bolts to rap anchor. (40')

F. Show and Tell 5.10a
T. Goss, E. Jones
Show me some choss and I'll
tell you to stay off it. Four bolts
to rap anchor. (40')

G. The Other White Meat 5.7*
T. Phillips, A. Seals
Low angle corner crack.
Medium to large pro. Walk off
to descend. (40')

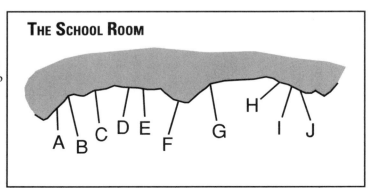

THE SCHOOL ROOM

AREAS OF SPECIAL INTEREST

THE RED CLIFFS DESERT RESERVE

With the rapid growth of the southwestern Utah region have come many challenges to both the local human and wildlife populations. As housing developments and the infrastructure to support them occupied more and more of the landscape around St. George, the habitat available for several species began to feel the pressure of this area's popularity.

The restrictions concurrent with the placement of these animals on threatened or endangered species lists caused concern over the future of the region. After several years of negotiation, the Red Cliffs Desert Reserve was formed in 1998 to provide and conserve habitat for threatened species such as the Desert Tortoise (*Gopherus agassizii*), Gila Monster (*Heloderma suspectum*) and Red Tailed Hawk (*Buteo jamaicensis*). The charter of this reserve also allows for recreation opportunities that do not negatively impact the protected species, or damage the habitat of those species.

So what does this mean to us as climbers? First and foremost, we should strive to have as little impact, and leave as little trace as our recreation allows. Litter, loud music, obnoxious behavior, bonfires and cross-desert travel are all inconsistent with climbing in this area. Probably the biggest impact we have on these areas is just getting to them. It is vital that you use the described approaches for each area, and stay on the trails. Once at an area, rack up, belay and otherwise hang out at the impacted site at the base of the climb. At several crags we have cordoned off climbing areas, and begun re-seeding programs to restore the vegetation to its original condition. Your cooperation in this effort is vital if we are to retain the privilege to climbing in these places.

Several developed climbing areas are within the boundaries of the reserve, and as such are subject to special regulations and rules regarding our behavior. At press time the climbing situation at crags on the Red Cliffs Reserve is in flux. It would be best to check with a local climbing shop for the current situation prior to climbing in the reserve.

IRON COUNTY CRAGS

The drive north on I-15 from St. George provides a geology, geography and biology lesson all rolled into one. Leaving behind the creosote and mesquite of the Mojave, the highway threads its way between the lacolith of the Pine Valley Mountains to the west and the Hurricane Cliffs to the east. As the elevation increases, the Great Basin ecosystem begins to assert itself as more sage and juniper appear along the road, while on the cliff tops, fir and aspen dominate.

The diversity of rock types in Iron County is astounding. Within a twenty mile radius of Cedar City there are limestone, quartz monzonite, quartzite conglomerate cobbles, welded tuff and basalt climbing areas. It is both this variety and cool summertime temperatures that draw climbers to the region. In fact, while many lower areas bake in the Southwestern Utah heat, climbers at The Overlook have been known to need fleece jackets in July.

CHART OF ESSENTIAL CRAG INFORMATION

LOCATION	TYPE OF STONE	SUMMER SHADE	WINTER SUN
10 Mile Wall	limestone	2 p.m. to sunset	10 a.m. to 12 p.m.
Animation Wall, The	limestone	sunrise to 2 p.m.	1 p.m. to sunset
Black and Tan Wall	limestone	3 p.m. to sunset	sunrise to 12 p.m.
Black Rocks N Wall	basalt	sunrise to 4 p.m.	never
Black Rocks S Wall	basalt	5 p.m. to sunset	8 a.m. to sunset
Bluff St. Cracks	sandstone	sunrise to 12 p.m.	2 p.m. to sunset
Boy Wall, The	limestone	sunrise to 2 p.m.	3 p.m. to sunset
Cathedral, The	limestone	sunrise to 7 p.m.	never
Cetaceam Wall, The	limestone	2 p.m. to sunset	10 a.m. to 12 p.m.
Chuckawalla	sandstone	sunrise to 12 p.m.	11 a.m. to sunset
Cone, The	welded tuff	5 p.m. to sunset	sunrise to sunset
Cougar Cliffs	sandstone	sunrise to 12 p.m.	12 p.m. to sunset
Crawdad Canyon N	basalt	sunrise to 1 p.m.	3 p.m. to sunset
Crawdad Canyon S	basalt	2 p.m. to sunset	sunrise to 3 p.m.
Diamond, The	limestone	sunrise to 2 p.m.	1 p.m. to sunset
Dutchmans Draw	limestone	almost none	sunrise to 4 p.m.(some)
Gorilla Cliffs	limestone	sunrise to 5 p.m.	never
Graveside Matter, The	limestone	sunrise to 2 p.m.	12 p.m. to 4 p.m.
Green Valley Gap	sandstone	5 p.m. to sunset	8 a.m. to sunset
Iron Mine, The	welded tuff	sunrise to 2 p.m.	11 a.m. to 5 p.m.
JB Crag	limestone	11 a.m. to sunset	never
Kellys Rock	limestone	sunrise to 10 a.m.	never
Logan Wall, The	limestone	1 p.m. to sunset	never
Overlook, The	welded tuff	sunrise to 12 p.m.	snow-covered area
Parawan Gap	quartzite conglomerate	4 p.m. to sunset	11 a.m. to 4 p.m.
Pioneer Park (bouldering)	sandstone	sunrise to 12 p.m.	1 p.m. to sunset
Pocket Rocks	welded tuff	sunrise to 10 a.m.	sunrise to sunset
Point, The	sandstone	5 p.m. to sunset	8 a.m. to sunset
Prophesy Wall	sandstone	sunrise to 12 p.m.	1 p.m. to sunset
Running Scared, The	basalt	sunrise to 2 p.m.	snow-covered area
Shinobe	quartzite conglomerate	sunrise to 12 p.m.	9 a.m. to 5 p.m.
Simian Complex, The	limestone	sunrise to 5 p.m.	never
Snake Pit, The	limestone	never	sunrise to 5 p.m.
Snow Canyon	sandstone	sunrise to 12 p.m.(most)	12 p.m. to sunset (most)
Soul Asylum, The	limestone	3 p.m. to sunset	sunrise to 12 p.m.
Sprocket Rocks	welded tuff	sunrise to 10 a.m.	sunrise to sunset
Sumo Wall, The	limestone	2 p.m. to sunset	10 a.m. to 12 p.m.
Turtle Wall	sandstone	2 p.m. to sunset	sunrise to 1 p.m.
VRG Mentor side	limestone	sunrise to 4 p.m.	4 p.m. to 6 p.m.
VRG Sun Cave side	limestone	4 p.m. to sunset	sunrise to 4 p.m.
Wailing Wall, The	limestone	sunrise to 4 p.m.	never
Warm Up Wall	limestone	3 p.m. to sunset	sunrise to 12 p.m.

Camping and Bivy Sites

Climbers are a rather thrifty bunch accustomed to ascetic lifestyles. The ability to create a three course meal out of condiment packets and packing peanuts is not one taught at any finishing schools. So it comes as no surprise that choice campsites are prized possessions, guarded and negotiated over like Israeli settlements in the Holy Land. Fortunately there are a wealth of camping and bivy options within a short distance of most of the climbing areas in this guide.

To most climbers, guidelines on how to treat the land and leave minimum impact on a campsite need not be said. However, an underclass of miscreants and swine certainly exists who probably need to be told. The following guidelines are for people like the idiot who drained his oil into the dirt, and left the filter in the middle of the pool at the Black Rocks parking area.
- Leave the area nicer, that is less littered, than you found it.
- Do not cut live trees for campfires.
- Use established fire rings where possible.
- Avoid trampling alpine meadows in the mountains, and cryptobiotic soil (that's desert crust for you rednecks) in arid areas.
- Respect private property, and get permission before camping there.

Utah Hills
On the road to Gorilla Cliffs at the 1.5 mile mark there is a nice site on the left. The parking area for the Soul Asylum is also a good bet.

Welcome Springs
The cattle pens at the end of the 2WD road, or the wash just past the Sumo Wall is nice if no threat of thunderstorms exists.

The Woodbury Road Crags
At the Black and Tan parking area, or on the left when driving in at the 3.0 mile mark.

The VRG
The Cedar Pockets Recreation Area offers pay camping with restrooms about 3.0 miles north of the crags. There are also bivi sites on the other side of the interstate in this same location.

The Dutchman Draw area
Virtually anywhere flat not currently occupied by a cow or cow shit. There is a nice bench at the lefthand turn towards the Phalanx of Will, but again not a good place to be in a flash flood.

West Cedar Crags
Several nice flat sites are located along the maze of dirt roads to the trailhead for Pocket Rocks. Farther in reduces the highway noise, and ensures that you're on public land. The Iron Mine parking area or along the last dirt road are also good bets for solitude.

East Cedar Crags
A National Forest campground about 5.0 miles up the canyon offers developed camping for $7.00 per night. Across the street, and a bit up canyon from the SUU cabin, there are some dirt roads with low-key bivi sites available.

Parowan
The parking area across the road from Shinobe is a nice grass-covered field, but may be covered with sheep shit from the local hooved "locusts", depending on the season.

Brian Head

The Overlook and Sidney Valley have numerous regularly used campsites, both at the climbing area and along the dirt roads lacing the area.

The Running Scared Wall

The woods along the dirt road to the north of the wall offer numerous camping opportunities.

St. George Crags

Probably the most problematic camping due to their proximity to town, and location on the Red Cliffs Reserve. There are occasionally campers right in the parking areas at Chuckawalla and Black Rocks, but a much better option is just west of Green Valley, down the hill just prior to entering the Gap. For those interested in nicer sites, free camping is found about 0.25 mile downstream of Gunlock Reservoir along the Santa Clara River. Snow Canyon has a state-of-the-art campground with showers, volleyball court, and electricity. The fee for such luxuries is a stiff $14.00 per night, but this includes park entrance fee.

Veyo

Primitive camping is to be had at Upper Sand Cove Reservoir across the street from the Prophesy Wall. Veyo Pools offers group campsites for $20.00 per night, or walk-in sites for $10.00 per night.

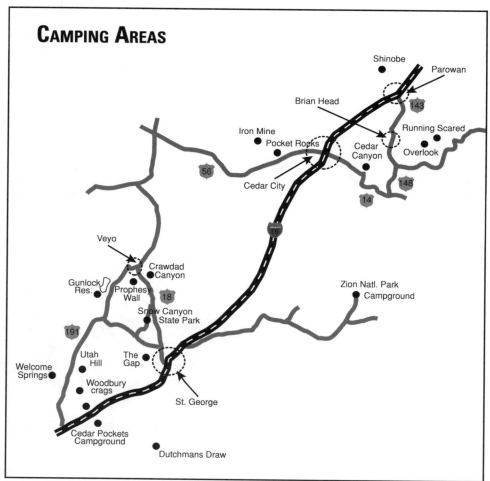

CAMPING AREAS

ROUTE AND CRAG INDEX